SERGEI PROKOFIEV'S
Alexander Nevsky

Oxford KEYNOTES
Series Editor KEVIN C. KARNES

SERGEI PROKOFIEV'S
Alexander Nevsky

KEVIN BARTIG

OXFORD
UNIVERSITY PRESS

Library of Congress Cataloging-in-Publication Data
Names: Bartig, Kevin author.
Title: Sergei Prokofiev's Alexander Nevsky / Kevin Bartig.
Description: New York, NY : Oxford University Press, [2017] |
Series: Oxford keynotes | Includes bibliographical references and index.
Identifiers: LCCN 2017006985 | ISBN 9780190269562 (hardcover : alk. paper) |
ISBN 9780190269579 (pbk. : alk. paper)
Subjects: LCSH: Prokofiev, Sergey, 1891-1953. Aleksandr Nevskiĭ (Cantata) |
Prokofiev, Sergey, 1891-1953. Aleksandr Nevskiĭ (Motion picture music)
Classification: LCC ML410.P865 B37 2017 | DDC 781.5/42092—dc23
LC record available at https://lccn.loc.gov/2017006985

9 8 7 6 5 4 3 2 1
Paperback printed by Webcom, Inc., Canada
Hardback printed by Bridgeport National Bindery, Inc., United States of America

Series Editor's
INTRODUCTION

OXFORD KEYNOTES REIMAGINES THE canons of
Western music for the twenty-first century. With each
of its volumes dedicated to a single composition or album,
the series provides an informed, critical, and provocative
companion to music as artwork and experience. Books in
the series explore how works of music have engaged listeners, performers, artists, and others through history and
in the present. They illuminate the roles of musicians and
musics in shaping Western cultures and societies, and they
seek to spark discussion of ongoing transitions in contemporary musical landscapes. Each approaches its key work
in a unique way, tailored to the distinct opportunities that
the work presents. Targeted at performers, curious listeners, and advanced undergraduates, volumes in the series
are written by expert and engaging voices in their fields,
and will therefore be of significant interest to scholars and
critics as well.

In selecting titles for the series, Oxford Keynotes bal-
ances two ways of defining the canons of Western music: as
lists of works that critics and scholars deem to have

articulated key moments in the history of the art, and as lists of works that comprise the bulk of what consumers listen to, purchase, and perform today. Often, the two lists intersect, but the overlap is imperfect. While not neglecting the first, Oxford Keynotes gives considerable weight to the second. It confronts the musicological canon with the living repertoire of performance and recording in classical, popular, jazz, and other idioms. And it seeks to expand that living repertoire through the latest musicological research.

Kevin C. Karnes
Emory University

CONTENTS

ABOUT THE
COMPANION WEBSITE

OXFORD UNIVERSITY PRESS HAS created a website to accompany *Sergei Prokofiev's Alexander Nevsky* that features a variety of related multimedia materials, including audio clips for all in-text musical examples. Many of these resources are integral to the volume itself or provide needed and useful context. As with all of the websites for Oxford Keynotes volumes, the reader is encouraged to take advantage of this valuable online information to expand their experience beyond the print book in hand. The reader is encouraged to consult this resource in conjunction with chapters 2 and 3 in particular.

www.oup.com/us/span
Username: Music4
Password: Book2497

The reader is invited to explore the full catalog of Oxford Keynotes volumes on the series homepage.
www.oup.com/us/oxfordkeynotes

ACKNOWLEDGMENTS

M UCH LIKE THE MULTIMEDIA work it celebrates, this book was in many ways a collaborative effort. Many institutions, archivists, librarians, colleagues, and friends made researching and writing the chapters that follow possible, and it is a great pleasure for me to thank them here. First and foremost, I owe a debt of gratitude to Kevin Karnes. A more enthusiastic and supportive series editor does not exist, and I will always be thankful he encouraged me to write this book. Suzanne Ryan and Norm Hirschy at Oxford University Press made everything about writing and publishing this book easier, and I consider myself fortunate to have worked with them. In Moscow, the staffs of the Russian State Archive of Literature and Art and the State Archive of the Russian Federation ensured that my research was as fruitful as possible. For financial support, I am grateful to Michigan State University's Humanities and Arts Research Program.

My debts to friends and colleagues are many. Annegret Fauser helped me get this book started, and I treasure her unflagging encouragement. Daniel Callahan, Maria

Cristina Fava, Carol Hess, Naum Kleiman, Katie McEwen, Vladimir Orlov, Marcie Ray, Svetlana Savenko, Doug Shadle, Svetlana Sigida, Daniel Tooke, and Elina Viljanen all helped in different ways, from reading parts of the text to sharing sources with me. Elena Tchougounova-Paulson was always ready to answer my questions about her native language and Chapter 6 would not be as rich had William David Brohn not answered my many questions about his reconstruction of *Alexander Nevsky*'s score so thoroughly. Marina Frolova-Walker and Patrick Zuk both read a draft of the entire manuscript, and their wisdom and insights made the final book much better. Finally, Alicia Levin, Sarah Long, and Russell Schwab patiently listened to me ramble on about this book and, being the great friends they are, distracted me when I most needed it. Thank you, all of you.

SERGEI PROKOFIEV'S
Alexander Nevsky

CHAPTER 1

ORIGINS, ADVANTAGES, ANXIETIES

I N LATE DECEMBER 2008, viewers across Russia tuned in to *Name of Russia*, a television program that aired on the state-owned news channel Rossiia-1. Taking their cue from contests such as *100 Greatest Britons*, the show's creators challenged their viewers to identify the most significant figure in Russian history. Votes poured in via telephone, text message, and internet. The results stunned many: in the top twelve, the dictator Joseph Stalin stood in third place. Some viewers expressed satisfaction, perhaps longing for past military might. Others suspected rigged votes of media sensationalism and pundits scrambled to explain Soviet nostalgia to bemused Westerners. Amid all of the chatter over a murderous dictator's merits and drawbacks, the first-place winner went unnoticed and unchallenged.

Reporting on the result, the BBC identified the winner as Saint Alexander Nevsky (1221–63), a prince who "fought off European invaders in the 13th century to preserve a united Russia."[1] The announcement posted to *Name of Russia*'s website credited him with "might," "patience," and "endurance," qualities for which he had been canonized.[2] Here Alexander peers out at readers from a thumbnail image lifted from an uncredited painting, his battle gear shining in the sunlight and a red handkerchief tied around his neck. But he hardly resembles the many medieval icons that bear his image; rather, he looks uncannily like the Soviet actor Nikolai Cherkasov, a personal favorite of the third-place winner, Stalin (figure 1.1).

These connections are not coincidental. Pavel Korin, the Soviet artist who painted the image on *Name of Russia*'s website during the depths of the Second World War, was aware his audience knew nothing of medieval iconography. They did, however, know Sergei Eisenstein's *Alexander Nevsky*, a 1938 film that dramatized a chapter in Alexander's

FIGURE 1.1   Pavel Korin's painting of Alexander Nevsky (1943) as it appeared on a 1967 Soviet postage stamp. Wikimedia Commons.

life of state defense. Stalin loved the film, particularly the portrayal of the title role by—perhaps this will come as little surprise—Nikolai Cherkasov, who is seen in figure 1.2. "I'll find an actor," Eisenstein supposedly joked to his colleague Mikhail Romm, "and cast him as Alexander Nevsky, and the whole world will soon believe that the real Nevsky was just like my actor."[3] And so it was. When Korin began his portrait three years later, Eisenstein's film had transformed the popular imagination of Stalin's Russia, elevating a little-known historical figure to a symbol of state defense, wartime valor, and national identity. The film's scenario, created by Eisenstein (1898–1948) and the writer Petr Pavlenko (1899–1951, another Stalin favorite), transformed a complex and spotty historical record into a

FIGURE 1.2   Production photo. Sergei Eisenstein is second from left; Nikolai Cherkasov is fourth from the left. Eduard Tissé, Eisenstein's cameraman, is standing. RGALI f. 1923, op. 1, ed. khr. 446, l. 14.

simple, rousing narrative. It begins with crisis: a band of marauding Teutonic Knights has invaded Russian lands and sacked the city of Pskov. Citizens of nearby Novgorod, led by Prince Alexander, gallop to the rescue. On April 5, 1242, they confront the knights on a frozen lake, an event that became known simply as the Battle on Ice. Alexander and his forces repel the knights, eventually forcing them into a retreat across the frozen lake. The ice breaks under the weight of the knights' heavy armor, and the invaders sink to their deaths. Alexander, victoriously entering liberated Pskov, proclaims, "He who comes to us as a guest, let him come with no fear. But he who comes to us with a sword shall die by the sword." It took little imagination for viewers in 1938 to see that the film was an allegory; Eisenstein himself saw little difference between Nevsky's plight and contemporary "German aggression" and "fascism."[4] By 1938, Hitler's crescendoing belligerence weighed on minds across the European continent, and Alexander's concluding proclamation echoed as a statement of contemporary foreign policy long after the theater lights came up. It also stirred patriotism and, by mobilizing historical imagery through such emotional appeals, granted the USSR a long, legitimizing past. Produced in a country that built its postwar identity on wartime sacrifice and victory, *Alexander Nevsky* survived the Stalin era, as present for Soviet citizens at the height of the Cold War as it was for the *Name of Russia* voters in the Putin era.

Following *Nevsky*'s Soviet premiere on December 1, 1938, viewers were as likely to recall Alexander's proclamation as they were to hum a tune from the film's musical score, composed by Sergei Prokofiev (1891–1953). "I remember how happy Sergei Sergeevich was," recalled the composer's first wife Lina, "when ... I told him how some boys playing war ran up a hill loudly singing 'Arise, Ye Russian People' [one of *Nevsky*'s choruses] and then went off 'on the attack.' "[5] This accessibility and popular resonance was a coup for Prokofiev, who quietly hoped his music for *Alexander Nevsky* might bring the public acclaim he had largely lacked since 1936, when he relocated to Moscow after nearly two decades abroad. He had every reason to be pleased, as contemporary writers hailed the *Nevsky* score as dramatic yet immediately accessible and attractively tuneful. Audiences have agreed ever since, enjoying the work both as part of Eisenstein's film and separately, as a cantata (op. 78), a half-hour, seven-movement affair for large orchestra, chorus, and mezzo-soprano, which Prokofiev arranged for concert performance in 1939 to capitalize on the film's success.

From the beginning, Prokofiev's *Nevsky* music entered the critical and popular imagination in different forms. In theaters, audiences perceived it as a collaborative work, one intimately connected to image. Decoupled from that specificity in the concert hall, the music proved malleable, its meaning reconfigured to suit different circumstances and times. As a generalized narrative of struggle and victory, it resonated deeply with audiences in England and the United States during the Second World War, remaining a repertory staple on both sides of the Iron Curtain long after the war turned cold and allies became enemies. In Prokofiev's homeland, the sacralization of the war made the cantata an instant classic, a historical document as much as a model of musical craft. At the height of the early Cold War, the Soviet musicologist Israel Nestyev reminded his readers that the music had galvanized soldiers during the Siege of Sevastopol (1941–42).[6] At the same time in the West, it was "one of the composer's finest creations ... a work of great dignity and power," despite having "originated as motion-picture music." Such was the description of David Ewen, an American critic of Austrian birth, which seems to imply we can forget the agitprop, as this is a great work of *art* music.[7] The music served wildly different ends. In 1960, for example, as Soviet music students pored over the *Nevsky* Cantata as a model of "correct" Soviet composition, Fritz Reiner recorded the work with the Chicago Symphony to show off RCA's high-fidelity capabilities. Other reformulations were more subtle. The famous half-step figure of impending attack in Steven Spielberg's *Jaws* (1975) is the same as that which underscores the Teutonic Knights' advance in *Nevsky*. Echoes of *Nevsky*'s music turn up in Aleksander Ford's *Krzyżacy* (1960), a historical drama made in communist Poland, as much as they do in Sam Raimi's Hollywood blockbuster *Darkman* (1990). Prokofiev's music has even been appropriated wholesale, such as in Pier Paolo Pasolini's film *The Gospel According to St. Matthew* (1964), where it accompanies Herod's slaughter of the innocents. Perhaps the most fascinating reconfiguration began in 1987, during the heady days of Mikhail Gorbachev's reforms. Prokofiev's original film score, reconstructed and performed live to a showing of the film, became a smash hit as a "film-concert," repeated well over fifty times by major orchestras by the time the Soviet Union fell apart. As the country that first cradled these images and sounds crumbled and ideologies and contexts shifted once again, *Nevsky* shuttled around the world, from the Dorothy Chandler Pavilion in Los Angeles to the ruins of Pompeii.

Prokofiev's *Alexander Nevsky*—a film score, a cantata, a film-symphony—is fertile ground for asking both musicological and cultural-historical questions. For one thing, examining *Nevsky*'s creation affords a glimpse into the popular culture of Soviet Russia a generation after one historical rupture (the Revolution of 1917) and teetering on the brink of another (the Second World War). Placing Prokofiev into this context—the goal of this chapter and the two that follow—brings familiar tropes into play. For example, one of the most widely used English-language music history textbooks reports that Prokofiev's music "was relatively simple, immediately comprehensible, full of melody, and often folklike in style," evidence that Prokofiev "fully adapted to the doctrine of socialist realism," an ostensibly state-mandated aesthetic policy that Stalin's government wielded to discourage autonomous experimentalism in the arts.[8] In other words, had authorities not meddled in artistic affairs, Prokofiev's stylistic trajectory might have been quite different. Herein is the neat binary of state-versus-artist long popular in the West, one from which other binaries—oppressor-versus-victim, compromised art-versus-unfettered creativity—follow. Prokofiev, to be sure, wrestled with the conservative creative space of his homeland. More often, as we will see, he wondered if he could write music for *any* mass audience and still consider his work "art," a concern hardly specific to Soviet Russia. As we consider *Alexander Nevsky*'s genesis and creation, we might ask to what extent Prokofiev triangulated the limitations placed upon him by the political context in which he worked with the expectations of his collaborators (*Nevsky* was a multimedia work, after all) and his own aesthetic convictions, many of which had wide international resonance. In terms of reception, the ways in which musicians, critics, scholars, and listeners have encountered Prokofiev's *Alexander Nevsky* in its various forms are surprisingly understudied given the work's popularity. *Alexander Nevsky* has been denounced, for instance, as Stalinist triumphalism even as crowds of thousands at the Hollywood Bowl raved at its sounds and images. To explore the music's reception, as we will do in the second half of this book, is to uncover the ways in which time, place, political concerns, and critical traditions mediate the meaning of an iconic work like Prokofiev's.

But that is getting ahead of the story. We can begin with some basic questions concerning *Alexander Nevsky*'s creation. Why, for instance, would Soviet authorities want to support a historical film about a long-dead prince about whom most knew precious little? And, perhaps more to the point, why would Prokofiev want to compose for such a film?

RUSSIAN PAST, SOVIET PRESENT

On December 7, 1944, a small group of directors, actors, and writers shuffled into a viewing hall at Mosfilm (the Soviet Union's leading film studio), where a pre-release version of Eisenstein's second sound film, part one of *Ivan the Terrible*, was loaded onto the projector. As the reels turned, they carefully scrutinized the director's work. When the lights came back up, they heatedly debated the film's merits, touching on issues ranging from acting to the historical basis of the plot. The latter in particular concerned one of the editors of the newspaper *Pravda*, Mikhail Galaktionov, who grew exasperated when his colleagues challenged the historical veracity of Eisenstein's work. Arguing that there could always be different artistic interpretations of the same historical event, he seemed to say that one would be foolish to look upon a feature film as a textbook. The writer Boris Gorbatov interjected that Soviet cinema boasted a number of films about the historical unifiers of medieval Rus (an East Slavic state) and modern Russia, including *Alexander Nevsky* and *Peter I*. Noting that a film dedicated to another unifier, Dmitri Donskoi, was in the works, he asked rhetorically how such films "affect our ordinary viewers emotionally." "Most importantly," he argued, "the idea of *Alexander Nevsky* was stirring. All viewers sense this. Why did Rus come together? Rus came together to smash the knights on Lake Chudskoe."[9] Here, in dialogue preserved on yellowed transcript pages, we glimpse the tension between the historical record and its rendering on-screen in historical film as an uncomplicated tale accessible to "ordinary" viewers (in Russian, Gorbatov's "ordinary" [*prostoi*] can also imply unsophistication). But that tale: Was it bowdlerized or stirring? Or, more to the point, disinterested or propagandistic?

Moreover, why discuss films about the distant past, of all things? This is as much our question as it was theirs, as in the 1920s and early 1930s, Soviet film largely addressed events in living memory, especially those connected to the advent and early years of Bolshevik rule. Eisenstein's famous *Battleship Potemkin* (1925) chronicled a 1905 naval mutiny against Tsarist authority, for instance. One of the most popular films of the early 1930s, *Chapaev* (1934), glorified a Red Army commander. But by the late 1930s, the more distant past had begun to enter theaters. Cinemagoers saw Nevsky, Donskoi, and Peter (who hailed from the thirteenth, fourteenth, and eighteenth centuries, respectively) as black-and-white Russian patriots projected onto screens, each adding bricks to the historical foundation of Bolshevik authority. As the Soviet present accrued a long Russian pedigree in this way, many watching from abroad wondered if a "great retreat" was underway in Soviet society, the films a symptom of a reactionary nationalism taking the place of Bolshevism's forward-looking internationalism.[10]

The reality was, of course, far more complex. Gorbatov's mention of "stirring" ideas points to a central concern of Soviet power since its inception. The Russian Revolution had promised a utopian world-to-come, one that had yet to materialize two decades into Soviet reality. Films like *Chapaev*, which applauded pro-Bolshevik heroism, inspired a kind of historically rooted patriotism that distracted from the everyday failures of Bolshevik rule. Lenin had famously dubbed film as "the most important of the arts" in the early 1920s. His assertion presaged a film industry that by the 1930s was firmly entangled with state concerns. Viewed from the perspective of those who sought to assert Soviet legitimacy, the turn to historical topics was pragmatic. Glorified heroes such as Peter the Great or Alexander Pushkin, the father of Russian literature, were well-known and safer subjects than the contemporary figures whom Stalin's purges could capriciously strike from history. As Kevin Platt and David Brandenberger have written, "Not only were the Peters and Pushkins arguably more familiar to average Soviet citizens than the Frunzes, Shchors, and other Bolshevik heroes ... but they were far easier to propagandize."[11] Indeed they were; the centenary of Pushkin's death in 1937, for example, featured lectures, reading groups, cultural events, and the chance to purchase a new edition of his collected works. In Moscow, venerable locales such as the Ostankino Palace, the right bank of the Moscow River, and the State Museum of Fine Arts were renamed in honor of the writer. The same year, Part 1 of Vladimir Petrov's *Peter I*, the Soviet Union's first historical blockbuster, appeared in theaters to great acclaim. Two years later, Mikhail Glinka's opera *A Life for the Tsar* (1836), an Imperial classic absent from stages since 1917, premiered at Moscow's Bolshoi Theater in heavily revised form and sporting a new title, *Ivan Susanin*, after the opera's central character, who sacrifices himself for Russia. Alexander Nevsky, the oldest figure brought out of cold storage, proved eminently useful during the late 1930s, a time when a connection between collective Soviet identity and the Russian past was forming. In addition to his victory over invading German knights, he and his army had successfully repelled encroaching Swedish forces at the River Neva in 1240 (the source of Alexander's appellation "Nevsky"). Elevated from prince of Novgorod to grand prince of Vladimir, Alexander maintained stability in the lands that would become northwest Russia until his death in 1263. As a figure known for state defense and little else, he was an exceptionally malleable hero for state propaganda.[12]

Eisenstein developed an international reputation amid these changes. In addition to *Potemkin*, he had made three avant-garde silent films on revolutionary subjects: *Strike* (1925), *October* (1928), and *The General Line* (also known as *The Old and the New*, 1929). He wrote extensively about film theory, especially how montage—the juxtaposition of images through editing—could influence audience emotion or create non-narrative visual associations and metaphors. His studio work floundered in the increasingly conservative 1930s, however. Projects he tackled between 1930 and 1937 all failed, either for lack of support or, in the famous case of *Bezhin Meadow* (1936), because of censoring on ideological grounds. Politburo members halted production of this film, a drama based on the purportedly true tale of a boy who denounced his anti-Soviet father, vilifying it as "anti-artistic and politically groundless."[13] The attack was a warning shot across the bow, one meant to demonstrate film production was subservient to government aims, as Oksana Bulgakowa and others have shown.[14]

Eisenstein's career was in peril, but a tense Politburo vote supervised by Stalin allowed the director one more chance. His options were limited. By the late 1930s, production quotas dictated the type of films that could be made, and artistic councils (such as the one we observed at the outset of this section) presided over their execution.[15] The scenario for *Alexander Nevsky*, which Pavlenko had completed and sold to Mosfilm already in early 1937 under the title *Rus*, was, for all intents and purposes, assigned to the director. Eisenstein could be casual with respect to fidelity to the historical record, as we have already noted in his quip to Mikhail Romm. Yet the specialist journal

Kino reported that Eisenstein had, in preparation for the production, pored over "historical materials and monuments of the thirteenth century in Moscow, Leningrad, Novgorod, and Pereslavl-Zalessky," research necessary because "in literature, iconography, and museums the thirteenth century is poorly represented."[16] Here, again, we glimpse a familiar tension between historical veracity and contemporary function. The Slavicist Evgeny Dobrenko has written that the resurrection of historical figures and their adaptation to the needs of Soviet patriotism was akin to assembling a museum exhibit, with the artifacts of history pieced together to make a stirring narrative to which only the exhibit itself can testify. This cinematic museum served an outsized role in fixing historical interpretations at a time when public discourse was increasingly circumscribed.[17] It also provided a canvas for collective experience. As James von Geldern, a historian of Russian culture, has suggested, by applauding resolute historical figures, audiences "could express support for strong executive power," just as their revulsion at traitors and enemies could be akin to "denounc[ing] the treachery of Trotskii and others."[18] Viewers of *Alexander Nevsky* applauded state unity, as Gorbatov would have us believe, and in that way also supported the leadership of Stalin. But he and his colleagues first viewed the film in 1938, two months after Germany invaded the Sudetenland and only weeks after Kristallnacht, the pogrom that many consider the beginning of the Holocaust. Nobody, not least Eisenstein, hid the fact that the "stirring" film would whip audiences into an anti-German frenzy. The thirteenth century told a tale of the twentieth; Nevsky's victory over his aggressors would also be Stalin's. Moreover, topical planning helped those of Gorbatov's "ordinary" viewers who might miss these connections: *Alexander Nevsky* opened alongside the documentary drama *If Tomorrow Brings War*, an assemblage of military practice footage that trumpeted the USSR's readiness.

Our story thus far is one of unabashed state propaganda. Although top-down bureaucratic directives encouraged or even dictated the creation of a useable past in art, artists applied their talents to these topics for many reasons. Motivations ran the gamut from professional opportunism to the desire for a role in shaping state ideology. In a surprising number of cases, creative figures, despite working within a tightly regulated state apparatus, were excited to create what they understood as art with broad social relevance. Although the ideological content of this art was distinctly Soviet, drawing attention to the social functions of art was a trend that was hardly confined within Soviet borders. Having now invoked both artistic agency and a broader, international perspective, we should turn to Prokofiev. In 1938, after all, the forty-seven-year-old composer still maintained an international career and viewed his repatriation as a simple relocation of home base.

CONTINUITIES AND DISRUPTIONS

On the evening of June 30, 1925, Prokofiev, then a resident of Paris, dined with Alexander Benois, whom the composer knew as the designer for many of the productions mounted by Serge Diaghilev's Ballets Russes. Benois convinced Prokofiev to see his most recent project, the set for

Abel Gance's epic film *Napoléon* (1927). Prokofiev later documented the visit in his journal:

> It was the first time I had been on a movie set, and I found it most interesting. A set had been erected inside an enormous barn, or hall, representing a room in Corsica. A very insignificant scene was being filmed, but this did not prevent it having to be started over again from the beginning five times. Three cameras were being used, the director yelled through a megaphone, but the main thing was the incredibly blinding illumination from a whole battery of lights focused on the acting area. I was amazed that the actors could tolerate such an intensity of radiation: I was standing in shadow, but the lights still made my eyes water. I was told that it is much more interesting when they are filming crowd scenes with three hundred people.[19]

At the time, Prokofiev's professional life was filled with ballet, an art form whose scale was far more modest than that of Gance's colossal undertaking. He was impressed. However, when he learned that fellow émigré composer Nikolai Tcherepnin was writing music for such productions, Prokofiev likened him to a "first-class railway carriage that has left the rails and shunted into a siding." "Because he is not getting any significant commissions," Prokofiev sniffed, "he is writing music for the cinema, hopelessly meretricious and woolly stuff."[20]

Why meretricious, particularly when cinematic productions clearly dazzled the composer? Backtracking a bit in Prokofiev's journal, we find that on the day Prokofiev visited the *Napoléon* set, his morning work session had been interrupted by another Russian émigré composer whom

Prokofiev often berated for what he felt was meretricious work. The visitor went by two names, Vladimir Dukelsky, a composer of ballets and symphonies, and Vernon Duke, a tunesmith who charmed Broadway audiences. Prokofiev encouraged the former, offering feedback on his music and introducing him to the elite circles in which he moved. Yet for all his success with listeners, the alter ego, Duke, failed to charm Prokofiev. When Duke's Broadway tune "I'm Only Human after All" rose to the top of the charts in 1930, Prokofiev dismissed Dukelsky as a commercial sellout. "No matter how you might pretend and prevaricate," he complained in response to his friend's protests, "the fact is that you like your half-respectable bread." [21] Duke was familiar with this crude accusation, the impresario Serge Diaghilev having said much the same years earlier, when he discovered that Duke had been arranging songs at a Paris cabaret for extra money. [22] For Prokofiev and Diaghilev, composing ballets and concert music for elite audiences—highbrow music, to use the parlance of the day—was an artistic calling, while writing popular songs (middlebrow music) was only a means to a paycheck. ("Lowbrow" referred to vernacular musics such as folk song.) They made it clear that followers of chic had no business writing for a broad, uncultured audience, whether on Broadway or in a movie theater. Thus from Prokofiev's perspective, Tcherepnin's middlebrow dalliances diverted his first-class carriage from the highbrow tracks that led to a respectable career.

This attitude is a point of continuity with nineteenth-century German Romantic aesthetics, the first to sacralize music as a profound and transcendent art created by the individual genius of a composer. Andreas Huyssen has written about the shadow the nineteenth century cast on the twentieth, and how it abetted a "Great Divide" between art and popular music. What Huyssen calls an "anxiety of contamination," a need to police the boundaries between highbrow and middlebrow, followed from this conceptual boundary.[23] Sergei Rachmaninov had "unbosomed himself in several much too flowery songs," Prokofiev told Dukelsky in a letter, and he "tried to assume a 'serious' mien, but resorted to such dry rot that he soon vanished from the scene altogether and remained in history as a composer of said flowery songs for the 'Greater public's' consumption."[24] To be sure, Prokofiev's conceitedness was legendary, but these words betray the inquietude of someone preserving his reputation among elite audiences and gatekeepers of musical institutions.

Dukelsky might have responded to Prokofiev in kind had he known his colleague had toyed with the idea of writing a film score at the same moment his "I'm Only Human after All" shot up the charts. The picture was *What a Widow!*, a romantic comedy starring Gloria Swanson. Although the Hollywood star dazzled her prospective composer, Prokofiev wondered in his journal if it was "possible to write simple music that is completely accessible to the masses and still stand to put one's name on it."[25] Yet he also quipped that Swanson's invitation was "splendid and smells of money."[26] Negotiations soured when Prokofiev requested a substantial fee, but he nevertheless was prepared to cross the Great Divide if the terms were right. By 1930, the potential of radio, sound film, and other emerging technologies was undeniable, and many composers shared Prokofiev's anxiety, if not his careerism. Aaron Copland, for instance, also wondered, "How are we to make contact with this enormously enlarged potential audience without sacrificing in any way the highest musical standards?"[27]

Teetering on the edge of the Great Divide, Prokofiev opted to straddle rather than leap, particularly while he was living in Paris prior to his 1936 repatriation. For the "millions" of listeners to whom Soviet order had brought music, for example, he proposed a "light-serious" musical style. "Finding a language for this music is not so simple," he asserted in a 1934 article in the Soviet newspaper *Izvestiia*. "Most importantly, it should be melodious, the melody furthermore simple and comprehensible, not resorting to a recycling or a trivial ditty.... The same goes for the compositional technique, for the manner of presentation; it should be clear and simple but not banal." He assured his readers that he had not forgotten "grand" music, which penetrated the "furthest development of musical forms."[28] Its elite audiences were implicit in its segregation from "light-serious" music. Examples from his own works were at the ready, with his symphonies (four to date) and the ballet *Sur le Borysthène* (1930–31) offered for sophisticated auditors. In the "light-serious" category was his first film score, a fleetingly brief collection of musical cues written for *Lieutenant Kijé* (1934), a Soviet parody of bureaucratic malfeasance during the reign of Russia's Pavel I. Prokofiev seemed to have answered the question he posed to himself in Hollywood four years earlier.[29]

Or was he just pandering to the authorities? Was Prokofiev backing away from his 1920s language—often dissonant, complex, and demanding—to curry favor with the conservative minds that held the purse strings of lucrative Soviet commissions? The profits from projects like *Lieutenant Kijé* did, after all, nudge Prokofiev ever closer to the Soviet Union during the mid-1930s. Yet for contemporary observers like Copland, there was little need for pandering. "It always comes as a surprise," he wrote in 1941, "to realize how little the essence of Prokofieff's music has changed during two decades.... One would have guessed that his musical style, so full of melodic invention and joie de vivre, would have been just what was needed in the Soviet republics."[30] He was right that lyricism and classical order characterize all of Prokofiev's works; in the early 1920s they had simply been dressed up in dissonances and overwrought textures. Casting that clothing off happened, moreover, well before the 1930s, and in Prokofiev's ballets, no less, as Stephen Press has documented.[31] "I think the desire which I and many of my fellow-composers feel, to attain a more simple and melodic expression, is the inevitable direction for the musical art of the future," Prokofiev reasoned, not to a Soviet official on the eve of his repatriation but to the *New York Times* music critic Olin Downes in 1930, the same year he eyed the "greater public" in Hollywood.[32]

Moreover, many shared his anxieties and convictions. Kurt Weill had bellowed in 1928: "Write this down! Music is no longer something for the few!"[33] A year later, the Mexican composer Carlos Chávez wrote (in a letter to his friend Aaron Copland) that he focused on "writing simple, melodic music ... that would be within the reach of the great mass of people and would eventually take the place of commercial, vulgar music then in great vogue, meant to incite the low passions."[34] And consider how Copland described his own music in the 1930s:

> The new mechanization of music's media has emphasized functional requirements, very often in terms of a large audience. That need would naturally induce works in a simpler, more direct style than was customary for concert works of absolute music. But it did not by any means lessen my interest in composing works in an idiom that might be accessible only to cultivated listeners.[35]

Different factors motivated these composers' pens—ideology, nationalism, economics—but insofar as accessible musical style was a common concern, the momentum that eventually brought Prokofiev to *Alexander Nevsky* had broad international resonance.

Prokofiev did, of course, tie his career to a land of increasing ideological control of the arts when he moved to Moscow in 1936. Creative production had been unionized in 1932, and union members had been charged with developing the doctrine of Socialist Realism, "a creative method based on the truthful, historically concrete artistic reflection of reality in its revolutionary development," to cite its official formulation.[36] Yet how music, arguably the most abstract of the arts, was to reflect a historically grounded reality was far from clear. As Marina Frolova-Walker has described, Socialist Realism in music emerged from the interaction between "broad directives from above," like the one we just observed, "the theorizing of musicians and critics, and the examples provided by new and recent compositions."[37] As composers concentrated on identifiable content, relying on implied or stated programs for instrumental works or favoring texted genres, they increasingly avoided modernist musical language that distracted from that message. They imitated successful works and in so doing gradually narrowed in on a cluster of positive qualities, chief among which were *dostupnost* (accessibility) and *konkretnost* (concreteness). In the increasingly xenophobic late 1930s, works inspired by nineteenth-century Russian nationalist classics, such as Nikolai Miaskovsky's Twelfth Symphony (1931–32), emerged as models. *Narodnost* (nationality) thus increasingly figured into the discussion. For many Soviet composers, these developments both reflected and emboldened already conservative tastes. Miaskovsky, to cite one example, had drifted toward a conservative style already in the 1920s.[38] When Prokofiev entered the scene a decade later, the stylistic remit of Soviet music had shrunk substantially, but to assume a tablet of rules landed at his feet is to imagine a clarity and regimentation that did not exist in reality.

Film music might seem a gift in this context, with images and words supplying the all-important content or "concreteness." Yet even by the time Eisenstein invited Prokofiev to compose for *Alexander Nevsky* in 1938, the commissioning, discussion, and execution of film music was a studio concern, beyond the purview of the Composers' Union. While Prokofiev had to parade his concert works before fellow union composers, his *Nevsky* score emerged quickly and without any of the tortuous discussion and revisions to which his ballets and operas were subject. Perhaps he found it ironic that critics later held up the *Nevsky* Cantata as a Socialist Realist work par excellence while his studied efforts to please his concert-music colleagues, such as the banal song cycle *Songs of Our Days* (1937), fell flat. These critics, as we will see, credited Prokofiev with reanimating in *Nevsky* the best of Alexander Borodin, Nikolai Rimsky-Korsakov, and other nineteenth-century Russian composers. But Prokofiev had blasted colleagues for that very sort of accomplishment. "Why do our musicians imagine that they can eat only yesterday's bread and rotten beef?" he bellowed during a Composers' Union meeting in 1937.[39] Contradictions such as these suggest that *Nevsky*'s positive example to Soviet music emerged as much through collaboration with Eisenstein and responding to the film's plot and goals as it did by subscribing to theoretical expectations for Soviet music.

Reflecting on the social upheaval wrought by the Second World War, Copland argued that "composers are more needed by the government today than they realize. On the homefront, for instance, they can stimulate and inspire love of the country ... If the government needs music it should, in all its official dignity, help the composers produce it."[40] Does this not sound like *Alexander Nevsky*, a state-sponsored project with a similar homefront goal?[41] Yet for all of the similarities that seem to cut across geopolitical boundaries during the 1930s and 1940s, Soviet artists were expected to support a single, ideological point of view in a way that their Western counterparts were not. Eisenstein was, for all intents and purposes, instructed to make a film about Nevsky by bureaucrats who oversaw film production. In agreeing to compose its musical score, Prokofiev merged his artistic convictions with the aims of state politics. In Stalin's Russia, creative agency and ideological imperative were locked in a perpetual dance, neither fully leading. The nature of that dance, and the ways in which generations of observers have condemned, celebrated, or willfully ignored it, unfolds in the chapters that follow.

CHAPTER 2

CREATING A BLOCKBUSTER

IN THE SWELTERING DAYS of early July 1938, Prokofiev's driver delivered him to an immense lot near Mosfilm. There Eisenstein had trained his cameras on a rehearsal for the Battle on Ice, for which several hundred actors surged across a simulated snow of white paint and sand. Prokofiev later described the visit in a letter to his longtime friend Vera Alpers, crowing that he had "thrown himself into work" on *Nevsky*, half of which would be

> taken up with the Battle on Ice, which is being filmed during the summer, with an ice field of asphalt, glass, and white sand (snow) painted white. I've been to the filming a few times, and it's turned out wonderfully, though the horses behave badly and the "ice" has to be cleaned continuously.[1]

The realities of fake ice and real horses scarcely detracted from the massive scale of the production, which must have reminded the composer of his visit to the set of *Napoléon* more than a decade earlier. But Prokofiev had hardly thrown himself into work on *Nevsky*. He wrote to Alpers from the sunny hills of southern Russia, where he would spend the remainder of the summer attending to other projects. To date he had met with Eisenstein a handful of times and composed a single, five-minute musical passage, or cue, as they are commonly known to film composers. Nevertheless, an undertaking of such scale clearly dazzled him, and he was presumably pleased that *Nevsky* was earning a great deal of press. The heavy lifting came only in late September, when he worked with Eisenstein on an almost daily basis leading up to the film's completion in early November.

That brief but intense period of work has fascinated many. Cinema history knows few instances of a renowned director and a famous composer (of concert music, no less) working together so closely. Yet that period has left a surprisingly slim documentary trace; the many accounts of the collaboration in specialist and popular literature derive largely from post-production accounts by the director and composer that are far from objective.[2] Rather than retell the story from Prokofiev's or Eisenstein's perspective, we might take a step back and consider their work more broadly. Eisenstein had worked with composers before, and Prokofiev relied on skills he had already honed in his ballet and incidental music. In their collaboration, both stuck to established convictions and techniques as much as they adapted to each other. Looking at their work from this perspective also allows us to see the ways in which the

FIGURE 2.1   Sergei Prokofiev and Sergei Eisenstein, promotional photo.

collaboration, and indeed the whole *Nevsky* production, became a form of propaganda itself, one shoehorned into Stalinist ideals of productivity and progress.

EISENSTEIN'S MUSIC

When Soviet studios released the country's first sound film in 1931, Eisenstein had already built a career in silent film. Facing the advent of sound film he teamed up with Gavriil Popov (1904–72), a young Leningrad composer eager to advance his career in both concert and film music. The composer stuck by Eisenstein through a number of failed or unrealized sound films during the mid-1930s, culminating with *Bezhin Meadow* (see chapter 1). Popov had already impressed Prokofiev during the latter's 1927 tour of the USSR. Prokofiev promoted the younger composer's concert music in France, while at home a broad public had applauded Popov's music for the cinema, particularly his score for *Chapaev*, whose fame we have already noted. The film's international distribution blazoned Popov's name on screens across the world.

Popov is important to our story. He was Eisenstein's first serious composer-collaborator, and the documentary record of their work together provides a window onto the future Eisenstein-Prokofiev collaboration. Consider the following passage from a letter Popov wrote to his wife, for example. Here he describes Eisenstein's reaction to a musical cue he had just finished:

> I showed the score to Eisen[stein]. He was a bit confused because he couldn't perceive the chorus's intensity (it doesn't come off well on the piano; the triads and six-four chords are closely spaced). A quarrel started. He said that it occasionally sounded too cultured (for a "peasant" chorus). I tried to explain the gradual coarsening of the chorus's texture near the end of the cue, where the chorus sings in simple fifths, thirds, and octaves.... The quarrel was difficult and tedious because Sergei Mikhailovich ... found it difficult to express his views on the score's specifics. His musical assistant Obolensky (arriving in the midst of the dispute) quickly calmed Eisenstein down by complimenting my score.[3]

We can learn much from Popov's account. On the one hand, Eisenstein involved himself in the composer's work, which paralleled rather than followed filming. (By contrast, the majority of Popov's colleagues composed only after a director had assembled a rough edit of the entire film.) On the other hand, Eisenstein clearly lacked a common language with Popov, who prevailed despite the director's best efforts. Whether with Popov or, later, with Prokofiev, Eisenstein relied on a rich, if idiosyncratic, vocabulary to describe his auditory and visual impressions. Yet in this case, Eisenstein came around only when he heard the cue with Popov directing the studio orchestra and choir, the composer exaggerating "the character and acceleration" so that Eisenstein would sense that "the rhythm was there." [4] Since the 1920s, Eisenstein had spent long hours in the cutting room, carefully piecing together brief, individual shots to form a meaningful whole. As the edited film played, the frequent cuts between shots visually tapped out a rhythm. Eisenstein listened for a sympathetic temporal organization in Popov's music, one he could sense in the cutting room as he matched sound with image. This need was a practical symptom of Eisenstein's conviction that in sound film, image and music must develop from the same fundamental rules, despite their divergent perceptual planes. As he wrote in 1939, sound film presented a unity in which "one and the same principle will nourish every part, appearing in each of them with their own special qualitative distinctions," a type of theorizing that owed a great deal to the nineteenth-century German romantic idea of a unified, organic work of art (of which we will see more in chapter 4).[5]

Eisenstein staked a lot on this conviction. Questioning, for instance, why image should come before music in a sound film, he instructed Popov to compose a cue for scenes he had yet to film.[6] Popov tried to develop Eisenstein's qualitative demands—"to depict sadness, severity, harshness, to build it to an (almost) heroic drama"—in an approximately five-minute span, the director's only quantitative request. And, just as a composer might watch a film's rough edit before composing, Popov was known to plunk out his music on a studio piano before Eisenstein filmed. *Bezhin Meadow*'s prohibition sadly forestalled a full realization of this model, but Eisenstein hoped for the chance when he asked Popov to compose for *Nevsky*. Tucked away in one of Popov's letters to the director is a fleeting reference to why the collaboration never came to be. Describing his newest cue for *Bezhin Meadow*, Popov insisted:

> The broad masses of the Soviet intelligentsia (writers, artists, employees of *Izvestiia*, and even professional composers), the wives of writers, Hermitage employees, doctors, and directors of school theaters will recognize this music as comprehensible, classic in style, substantial, and memorable.[7]

The passage is dripping with sarcasm. Popov's First Symphony (1934), a piece he worked on for nearly seven years, had recently been criticized for its inaccessibility and banned from performance.[8] This development remained a black mark on Popov's résumé throughout the 1930s. It scared off Mosfilm's upper administration when the question of *Nevsky*'s composer arose; Prokofiev joined the production when it became clear to Eisenstein that Popov had been unofficially banned from the studio.

A NEW COLLABORATOR

Prokofiev visited Hollywood during a concert tour in early 1938, his first time back since negotiating with Gloria Swanson eight years earlier. This time it was Paramount that courted the composer, but his commitments in Moscow meant negotiations had to be tabled. The visit rekindled his interest in cinema, however, and when Prokofiev arrived back in the Russian capital, Eisenstein was waiting. The details of their first meeting in the spring of 1938 are lost to history, but *Nevsky*'s attractions for Prokofiev are not hard to imagine: work with a renowned director at the country's leading studio, a high-profile state project, and a twenty-five-thousand-ruble honorarium, an astonishing amount that exceeded even some directors' pay (due to *Nevsky*'s unusually generous budget, Prokofiev eventually received a total of thirty thousand rubles).[9] Unlike his waffling negotiations with Swanson, there is no evidence that Prokofiev thought twice about working with Eisenstein. The contract he signed obligated him to supply musical cues for the Battle on Ice by mid-June, before filming of the sequence began, while the remainder of the score would be due later in the fall, after Eisenstein completed shooting.

Planning began in earnest. Pavlenko's scenario, already subject to many revisions, had been transformed into a director's script, to which the poet Vladimir Lugovskoi (1901–57) had added texts intended for three vocal numbers. Eisenstein handed Prokofiev a copy of this eighty-four page document, containing indications for nearly seven hundred individual shots. As they read together, Prokofiev jotted down notes in the margin, a rare trace of the collaboration-in-progress. Significantly, Prokofiev noted none of the theoretical details that filled Eisenstein's planning notebook, particularly his desire to structure the film in discrete tableaus of "pure" music, "organized sound" (such as the tolling of bells), and speech.[10] By contrast,

Prokofiev's pen coursed over the page when it came to specifics, related in Eisenstein's characteristic qualitative style. The opening music, for example, should convey the "sounds of recent battle" and not sound "passive." [11] Music for the Novgorod sequence should be "pleasant" to accord with "a marvelous river view." The Germans' military horns were to screech "like an ice-covered sound, tearing." Going into battle, the trumpets should maintain a steady rhythm that would match the army's steady approach, but the sound must travel "straight into the ear" and be "more terrifying" than the previous iteration. Similarly, the rhythmic "wheezing" of the Russians' horses was to have an identical "rattle" in the music. (Eisenstein, perhaps inspired by the thought of sounds penetrating straight into the ear, suggested that this rattle might be enhanced by placing microphones closer to the flutes and oboes during recording). Conspicuously absent are references to musical specifics. The few exceptions stand out: Eisenstein suggested that musical mode (i.e., major and minor keys) might track the course of the battle, with a drooping minor-key passage ("the downfall of Germany") yielding to a major key that would align with Alexander's victory cry. He also suggested making narrative connections within the music, an instrumental version of the post-battle lament giving a premonition of destruction before the battle, for instance. Throughout this process, Eisenstein fired Prokofiev's imagination with sketches like the ones seen in figures 2.2 and 2.3, which he used to plan *Nevsky*'s mise en scène. [12]

None of this conversation with Eisenstein was remarkable for Prokofiev. Swap script for libretto and he could easily have been planning a ballet, that audiovisual genre in which he

FIGURE 2.2   One of Sergei Eisenstein's sketches of the Battle on Ice, dated
April 12, 1938, around the time of his first meetings with
Prokofiev. S. Eizenshtein, *Risunki* (Moscow: Iskusstvo, 1961).

excelled. His most recent, *Romeo and Juliet* (1935–36), featured
short musical numbers that correspond to specific events in
the ballet's plot. Moments of extended symphonic development are rare. Motives—short, recurring musical figures—
made narrative connections among these cues, which he
turned out on a near daily basis, just as he would later in the
year with *Nevsky*'s cues. And, perhaps most importantly, work
on ballets such as *Romeo and Juliet* equipped Prokofiev with
the imagination to compose highly descriptive music for an
audiovisual project still awaiting its visual element.

FIGURE 2.3   Sketch for the Battle on Ice, dated May 12, 1938.

Likewise, there is no evidence to suggest that Eisenstein's music-first approach surprised Prokofiev; the composer even boasted to a reporter later in the year that part of the film was beholden to his "musical design."[13] The scene in question was the first of the Battle on Ice, in which the Teutonic Knights advance on Alexander's forces. Prokofiev filled the corresponding pages in the script with notes, and it is clear Eisenstein had rhythm on his mind. Here music and image were to be united by rhythm and texture; Prokofiev, for instance, wrote "(1) at a trot; (2) new clatter / of swords / of hoofs / the texture becomes more complicated as details are added," all features his music was to convey.[14] Under the script's indication of "the clang of the knights' weapons," Prokofiev noted that Eisenstein "wants me to clang." Alongside these localized details was an overall increase in intensity: "The Knights [become] larger; strengthen until [shot] 399." At the end of the section, Prokofiev indicated an overall duration of five minutes, one of the only specific indications of timing in the script. He had his first assignment. During the first week of June, he demonstrated the result on Mosfilm's studio piano so Eisenstein could make a reference recording. At this point, the director issued no further requests.[15]

NEVSKY'S STYLISTS AND THE COAL MINER

While Prokofiev worked on this first musical cue, Eisenstein traveled to Novgorod to scope out the town's fifteenth-century fortress, where he planned to film many of *Nevsky*'s outdoor scenes. Taking in the structure's disrepair, Eisenstein realized the fortress could never serve as a convincing set. As he returned to Moscow, Mosfilm set builders scrambled to construct a suitable replica of the Novgorod fortress on a lot near the studio. The press spun this development as evidence of Mosfilm's resourcefulness and sophistication, quietly glossing over the hurried nature and expense of unplanned construction.[16]

Such disruption was cause for concern. Only one month earlier, a newly created Committee on Cinematography Affairs exercised its power over studios by scrubbing the productions of a large number of films, ostensibly to improve efficiency. Anxiety grew among Eisenstein's colleagues, particularly as the director planned to wait until winter to film *Nevsky*'s Battle on Ice, a sequence that accounts for nearly one-third of the film. Given the new and capricious oversight, finishing the film quickly and efficiently seemed wise.[17] Eisenstein's ever-resourceful cameraman Eduard Tissé (1897–1961) began experimenting. He coated a six-foot piece of scrap plywood with white paint and sand, which, with the help of camera filters, yielded a plausible icescape.[18] Thus an ambitious, seemingly foolhardy plan emerged: the Battle on Ice would be filmed in the middle of summer on an outdoor set of fake snow and ice. Rather than meeting further with Prokofiev, Eisenstein turned his attention to questions of simulated winter. Prokofiev's work was temporarily done, and, after surveying Tissé's experiment himself, he left the capital for the remainder of the summer.

What he observed before departing was remarkable (figures 2.4, 2.5). A crew covered nearly a tenth of a studio lot the size of six football fields with asphalt, dusting it with chalk as it cooled before applying paint and sodium silicate (so-called liquid glass). The "snow" lay in strips spaced fifty meters apart, which gave the impression that the entire lot was covered when filmed from a low angle (figure 2.6). For close-up scenes, Tissé used mirrors to reflect sunlight (and, after clouds rolled in, the rays of a five-thousand-amp spotlight) onto the fake ice. Throughout filming, Tissé turned the camera's crank manually at low speed, the slow frame rate yielding a rhythmic graininess that made lightweight studio props seem like real swords and shields. A special headache for Tissé and Eisenstein was simulating the Teutonic Knights' plunge through the ice. In the

FIGURE 2.4   Production photo showing the Mosfilm lot used for filming the Battle on Ice. The strips of fake snow are visible in the background. RGALI f. 1923, op. 1, ed. khr. 447, l. 4.

FIGURE 2.5   Production photo, Battle on Ice. RGALI f. 1923, op. 1, ed. khr. 447, l. 35.

FIGURE 2.6   *Alexander Nevsky*, Battle on Ice, showing Eduard Tissé's low
camera angle.

completed film, stuntmen drop into a twenty-five-meter-
wide pool filled with six tons of real ice, a special brigade of
lifeguards saving the actors from the fate of their historical
counterparts.[19]

More important to our story are the ways in which
Nevsky's future audiences learned about Tissé's and
Eisenstein's ingenuity. In the specialist publication *Kino*,
Tissé bragged that "not even in Europe or America has this
technique been used." Such efforts were, he suggested, the
"beginning of a grand experimental work."[20] Hyperbolic
or not, Tissé brought the language of technological sophistication to a project that was undeniably populist. Other
reports impressed readers with size and scale, claiming
some one thousand actors participated in the Battle on

FIGURE 2.7   Production photo during filming of Pskov sequence. RGALI
f. 1923, op. 1, ed. khr. 446, l. 36.

Ice, dressed in some twelve thousand individual costume
items ranging from shoes to chainmail.[21] More widely
praised in the press were the speed and efficiency of production. For instance, on September 3, the day Eisenstein
finished the Pskov sequence, a reporter marveled that the
collective had filmed over two hundred percent of their
daily goal of footage.[22] Another session resulted in over
three hundred percent, a "Stakhanovite clip," the reporter
described, likening the accomplishment to that of Aleksei
Stakhanov, a coal miner who in 1935 had exceeded his daily
quota by some fourteen times.[23] Soviet media, fixed on the
glorification of Stakhanov, highlighted similar claims of
superhuman feats, making them a fixture of Soviet public
discourse during the late 1930s. In other words, the *Nevsky*

production was being fitted into a well-established mythol-ogizing narrative, one that, however loosely it represented reality, primed the film's coming success in theaters. For instance, those close to the *Nevsky* production knew that Tissé and Eisenstein had a stormy collaboration, the cam-eraman sometimes directing when the director refused to come to the set. Likewise, those who read the technical reports in newspapers like *Kino* knew that organizational difficulties and shortages of raw materials in fact delayed speedy completion of *Nevsky*. Nonetheless, all of the media hype would directly impact the film's reception, as we will see in chapters 4 and 5.

VIEWING HALL, RECORDING STUDIO

Prokofiev reunited with Eisenstein only in September, after Eisenstein had completed all of *Nevsky*'s filming. For almost a month, they met regularly in a Mosfilm viewing hall late at night, the studio's poor electrical supply and lack of soundproofing preventing daytime meetings. They began to deviate in places from the plan outlined in the director's script they had hammered out some five months earlier: Eisenstein demonstrated largely unedited footage, and Prokofiev, supplied with visual inspiration, returned to his apartment on the east side of Moscow to draft the next musical cue. Back at the studio the next day, he made reference recordings at the piano for Eisenstein. The direc-tor later commented on Prokofiev's clocklike punctuality, but the amount of work involved seems to have surprised Prokofiev, who complained in a letter to Alpers that he was "bogged down up to my ears" in work on *Nevsky* and had to postpone other projects. "But," he added, "Eisenstein is magnificent, and it's a pleasure to work with him."[24]

How did Prokofiev work back in his apartment? The few sketches that survive in Prokofiev's archive provide evidence that his daily conferences with Eisenstein had, at least in some cases, yielded specific timings. Using precise tempo indications (expressed as beats per minute), Prokofiev could bracket off the appropriate number of measures needed to fill a precise span of time. He then sketched musical ideas in the allotted space, often exploring several different possibilities before drafting the cue. This method was familiar territory for Prokofiev: he had used the same blocking method as early as 1933 with *Lieutenant Kijé*, and it figured into at least some of the incidental music he composed during the mid-1930s as well.[25]

FIGURE 2.8   Sergei Prokofiev working in his apartment on Chkalov Street in Moscow in 1939, the year he completed the *Nevsky* Cantata. I. Nest'ev, *Prokof'ev* (Moscow: Gosudarstvennoe muzykal'noe izdatel'stvo, 1957).

While Prokofiev wrote, Eisenstein worked in the cutting room, often editing while referring to Prokofiev's reference recordings. In some cases, this process yielded striking moments of sight-sound interplay. At the beginning of the Pskov sequence, for instance, Eisenstein cut largely static medium-length shots slightly out of sync with strong musical pulses in Prokofiev's music. Only when the first long shot appears does the cut align with a strong musical accent (figure 2.9, [23:02]; timings refer to the 2001 Criterion edition of the film). The coincidence, placed squarely on a widely spaced chord, lends a strikingly aural dimension to the sudden readjustment of visual scale. The results are more underwhelming in other cases. Poor planning or simply the frantic pace of production forced Eisenstein to loop some of Prokofiev's cues repeatedly during the Battle on Ice

FIGURE 2.9   *Alexander Nevsky*, Pskov Sequence, initial long shot.

(e.g., the music beginning at 1:05:16). Eisenstein's approach certainly struck many as unorthodox; as we already noted, a composer generally started working only after the director demonstrated an edit of the entire film. As Copland described Hollywood practice, "At this showing the decision is reached as to where to add music, where it should start in each separate sequence, and where it should end." This showing and the timings for each cue, Copland added, were "all that the composer needs for complete security in synchronizing his music with the film."[26] Prokofiev had more than once balked at the time constraints that such a method placed on a composer; his piecemeal work with Eisenstein accommodated his typical schedule far better.[27]

The real novelty for Prokofiev was the recording process. Mikhail Rozenfeld, a reporter covering the production for the journal *Soviet Literature*, observed a rehearsal of the studio orchestra, across from which "a choir stood like troops on parade." "A preoccupied Sergei Prokofiev," he continued,

> paced between the orchestra and choir with the score in his hands. Suddenly the mighty choir began to sing: "Arise, ye Russian people ..." Already a month ago we heard highly promising reports of the music Prokofiev had written. But what the choir sang in the recording hall exceeded all expectations.[28]

Here Rozenfeld hands the Stakhanovite torch to Prokofiev. In his own description, Prokofiev, just like the cameraman Tissé, insisted on the technological sophistication of his work:

> We placed the brass in one studio and a choir in another; both performed their parts simultaneously. From each studio, a

wire ran to a booth where the recording took place, and where by simply pressing a button the sound of one or the other group could be magnified or diminished, depending on the demands of the action. We also recorded using three microphones, which demanded great skill in merging ("mixing") all three channels.[29]

This excerpt comes from a 1939 essay Prokofiev wrote for a collection on Soviet film, in which he also described experimental microphone placement. A "strong, mighty bassoon against the background of a barely audible trombone" resulted, for instance, from placing the microphone directly above the bassoonist. Likewise, when the brass played directly into the microphone, the resulting distortion was a "wonderfully dramatic effect" suited to the repellant Teutonic Knights.[30]

These effects are easy to miss in the film. The sound quality is appalling, as is the orchestra's performance, which is often ragged and out of tune. Tellingly, when *Nevsky* premiered in the USA, critics pounced on the sound quality, comparing it unfavorably to Hollywood films.[31] Yet there is some evidence that officials approved the film's release earlier than expected, possibly before a final, well-rehearsed version of the music track could be added (indeed, there even seem to be traces of Prokofiev's piano reference recordings, such as at the conclusion of the Germans' Mass [57:50]).[32] Poorly produced soundtracks were, in any case, common in Soviet films during the Stalin era. Standards had fallen so low by the end of the decade that an artistic council concluded that poor sound quality had ruined Lev Shvarts's score for *The Magic Pearl* (1941).[33]

Is this deficiency why Prokofiev asserted that composers had to take control of the possibilities of the recording studio rather than, as he put it in his essay, "entrusting the recording to the film factory's mercy"? "Even the most skilled sound technician cannot possibly handle the music as well as the composer himself," he insisted.[34] Yet we can find other composers, even those working in Hollywood, who said much the same. Copland once joked that he would never "call in an engineer to tune [his] piano."[35] Prokofiev and Copland composed musical *works*—ballets, symphonies, and other "discrete, perfectly formed, and completed products," to borrow philosopher Lydia Goehr's influential description.[36] For concert and stage works, the pages of a score preserved their intentions for performers to enact. In cinema, that unchanging product was a piece of film. That neither Prokofiev nor Copland relinquished their agency in shaping that final product betrays the highbrow values we observed in the last chapter. Indeed, here Prokofiev might have seen the difference between himself and Vernon Duke when it came to music for the masses: unlike his émigré compatriot's popular songs, dashed off quickly and turned over to the indifferent hands of the popular music industry for reworking, recording, and money-making, Prokofiev's *Nevsky* was "serious" music, shaped by the composer's individual genius from beginning to end.

By the time *Alexander Nevsky* premiered on December 1, 1938, Prokofiev had confronted a mass audience and had begun spinning rhetoric that preserved his place in high-art circles. With *Nevsky*, Eisenstein had at last finished a sound film, a populist work of propaganda that had been hyped for nearly a year in both the Soviet and international

FIGURE 2.10   A page of the *Alexander Nevsky* manuscript score Sergei
               Prokofiev gave to Sergei Eisenstein at the conclusion of their
               work together. The inscription reads "To dear and remarkable
               Sergei Mikhailovich and Alexander Nevsky, destroyers of swine
               (in singular and plural forms), SPRKFV, 20 Nov. [19]38." In
               Russian, the Germans' military maneuver (a cavalry wedge)
               was colloquially known as *svinia*, "the swine." In plural form,
               swine referred to those who had disrupted Eisenstein's career.
               Prokofiev's humor is dark; Eisenstein's chief opponent, the
               bureaucrat Boris Shumiatsky, had been executed months before
               at the height of the Great Terror. Sergei Eisenstein Museum.

press for the efficiency and technological sophistication
of its production. During that time, Russian society had
grown more closed off from the rest of the world and anti-
Western rhetoric had become a fixture of political discourse. The confluence of these factors presaged a complex
and often contradictory reception among critics and audiences both at home and abroad. But before we turn to that
story, a closer look at Prokofiev's music is in order.

CHAPTER 3

THE THIRTEENTH CENTURY IN SOUNDS

E ISENSTEIN THOUGHT A LOT about how best to portray the enemy in his new film. For *Nevsky* to inspire patriotism, it needed both heroic protagonists and convincing antagonists from without, ones whose foreignness frightened as much as their violence. As his planning notebooks filled with ideas, Eisenstein asked a Mosfilm assistant to gather information on Roman Catholicism, the confession that distinguished medieval Germans from Orthodox Russians. Soon a meticulously prepared sheaf of notes landed on the director's desk, furnishing him with Latin texts of the mass ordinary, penned in a gently sloping hand between typed commentary and Russian translations. The assistant aimed to impress, appending a bibliography of French- and German-language references and a selection of images culled from various sources, including one that Eisenstein used as the model for the portative organ Mosfilm technicians constructed to his specifications (figure 3.1). Judging by the assistant's commentary, Eisenstein already imagined the Teutonic Knights participating in a mass as true to the thirteenth century as possible, joining the bishop, for example, in the Gloria, Alleluia, and other sung portions of the mass.[1] The diligent assistant's name is not recorded, but it may well have been Boris Volsky (1903–69), *Nevsky*'s eventual sound engineer. He later recalled that Eisenstein requested that he "track down some examples of ancient psalms for the film's composer S. S. Prokofiev," a task that yielded "a small amount of musical material that dated from the thirteenth to the fifteenth centuries."[2] It seems Eisenstein also thought a lot about historical veracity and expected his new collaborator would too.

FIGURE 3.1 *Alexander Nevsky*, The Teutonic Knights' Mass.

SERGEI PROKOFIEV'S *ALEXANDER NEVSKY*

Prokofiev had other ideas. As Volsky recalled, rather than imitate an unfamiliar thirteenth-century musical practice, Prokofiev wanted "to deceive cleverly." Just as Eisenstein sensed that nobody knew much about Nevsky, Prokofiev knew that the music of the hero's world would be entirely foreign to audiences. In early June, he trekked out to Mosfilm to demonstrate his solution, which was more a grotesque parody of liturgical song than anything true to historical practice. There is repetition, absence of any memorable melody, intentionally awkward placement of the four distinct vocal lines, and a lugubrious tempo (44:13). Herein is Prokofiev's trickery, his vocal polyphony calling to mind liturgical practice while at the same time repelling the listener with its ugliness. Moreover, rather than use the mass texts Eisenstein had collected, Prokofiev used his own ungrammatical Latin text, "Peregrinus expectavi pedes meos in cymbalis" (A stranger I waited my feet on cymbals), its incoherence meant to convey the emptiness of the Catholic rite.[3] Prokofiev also demonstrated a simple sixteen-note fanfare that, together with the psalm singing, would be the Teutonic Knights' musical calling card in the film. No evidence survives that Eisenstein was unhappy with Prokofiev's decidedly ahistorical work.

Plunking out the Germans' music for Eisenstein on a studio piano, Prokofiev offered his answer to a vexing question, namely, what kind of music suits a cinematic chronicle of the distant past. Rather than hew to historical verisimilitude, he opted for music that would move a viewer emotionally, dressing it up with stylistic markers that suggest verisimilitude to a listener who might not know better. Such might seem standard practice to twenty-first-century cinemagoers, but Eisenstein's preparatory work should remind us that there were few precedents in 1938, particularly for Soviet filmmakers. As we turn to Prokofiev's music, we might consider in particular two questions that were presumably on the composer's mind as he worked with Eisenstein. How does one "deceive cleverly" the audience of a historical film musically? And, perhaps more importantly, how does one achieve the musical accessibility implicit in such a concern?

MUSIC TO ORDER

The directives Eisenstein gave his collaborator during their first meetings were, of course, one point of departure for Prokofiev. We can find their traces in the music, especially in the cue Prokofiev wrote immediately after poring over the script with Eisenstein (later titled "Swine," as a cavalry wedge maneuver was colloquially known in medieval Rus). Recall that Eisenstein wanted the music to evoke the "clang" of weaponry. In response, Prokofiev devised the passage shown in example 3.1. The gesture is obvious even if one does not read musical notation: in place of a melody, we have constant eighth notes grouped in twos, with differences of

EXAMPLE 3.1 *Alexander Nevsky*, "Clang" figure at beginning of Battle on Ice.

SERGEI PROKOFIEV'S *ALEXANDER NEVSKY*

register suggesting back-and-forth interplay of swords. Rapid upward figures (the small notes at the top) suggest the whoosh of a sword cutting through air. These and other gestures were the basis of the music's abundant "visuality," as Prokofiev himself later termed it.[4] To be sure, Eisenstein did not align these musical gestures with visual analogues, as might be done in a cartoon (think of the falling musical line paired with Wile E. Coyote's many plummets from cliffs, for example). Rather, example 3.1 documents Eisenstein's resolve that music and image must follow from the same fundamental idea, even if they are conceptually divergent in the completed film—thus the music Prokofiev composed in response to the "trot" and "clatter" of hoofs and swords, which features an insistent half-step figure (example 3.2)

EXAMPLE 3.2 *Alexander Nevsky*, Half-step motive that corresponds to the Teutonic Knights' advance.

that continues unabated for nearly four minutes (58:10–1:02:06) and in the *Nevsky* Cantata for more than six dozen measures. The regularity of this pattern audibly relates the inexorable advance of the Teutonic Knights; in the cutting room, Eisenstein decided to use Prokofiev's music alone in the soundtrack, without mixing in the actual clatter of hoofs. The rhythm is active and constant, but the melodic line never departs from its alternation of two pitches, a combination Prokofiev knew would induce tension.

In addition to these localized image-music resonances, Eisenstein requested repeated musical motives that would connect events and themes. For instance, as the camera trains over the destruction of Pskov early in the film, Prokofiev introduces a melody (27:24) that is echoed later in a lament intoned by a female voice following the Battle on Ice (1:24:36). Music connects analogous scenes of loss and destruction, subsuming them into *Alexander Nevsky*'s general themes of attack and defense. Far more often, however, Prokofiev repeats entire blocks of music to make such connections. For example, the cue that accompanies the scenes of recent battle with which the film opens ("Ravaged Rus" [2:16]) is the same as that immediately preceding the Battle on Ice (48:16), underscoring the general theme of abuse from without. Two large choral numbers, "Song About Alexander Nevsky" (3:47) and "Arise, Ye Russian People" (35:05) appear in four different instrumental versions later in the film.[5]

Localized gestures and large-scale formal construction were important means of ensuring comprehensibility, that quality demanded by both a mass audience and, of course, Socialist Realism. An uninitiated or inattentive viewer was, after all, more likely to sense the repetition of entire musical cues than fleeting motives. And, as we will see, Prokofiev himself claimed the score's visuality was a concession to comprehensibility, musical abstractness in his mind being a quality enjoyed by only sophisticated listeners. Yet there are more subtle vehicles for ensuring accessibility too. They involve stark rhythmic and stylistic contrasts, Prokofiev's answer to the "exaggerated simplicity" of Eisenstein's images and editing, to borrow David Bordwell's description.[6] "Daybreak," the cue that immediately precedes the eighth-note trotting motive we noted earlier, begins with a hollow blast of sound, with the strings opening a static space that spans a full four octaves—a feature visually evident in example 3.3—the wide spacing suggesting the

EXAMPLE 3.3 *Alexander Nevsky*, "Daybreak," mm. 1–4.

vastness of the frozen battlefield. Long, sustained tones as well as static, repeated pitches arrest any sense of forward motion. The half-step figure brings a sudden sense of movement that cleanly parses the battle's phases without the aid of dialogue. These moments presumably gratified Eisenstein, a director whose ear was keenly tuned to rhythm. *Nevsky*'s musical pacing impressed a number of critics because it drew atypical attention to the film's score.

Eisenstein's Soviet biographer Rostislav Iurenev groused that the prominence of Prokofiev's music during sequences devoid of dialogue and quick-paced visual montage felt too much like the arias of an opera.[7] We might imagine such a reaction would please Prokofiev, who insisted that mass music should be light but serious—popular "art," so to speak—as we noted in the last chapter.

At a private pre-release discussion of *Nevsky*, the director Vsevolod Pudovkin immediately sensed Prokofiev's efforts at musical accessibility. Admitting that he found Prokofiev "difficult to understand in his symphonic compositions," Pudovkin praised *Nevsky*'s clarity, especially the "two sharply opposing themes: one empty, disjunct, akin to a Catholic hymn—the German theme—and the magnificent, resonant, tuneful theme of the Russians."[8] Assigning antagonists and protagonists contrasting musical themes was hardly original. Mikhail Glinka divided invading Poles and Russians in his opera *A Life for the Tsar* (1836) with syncopated passages in triple meter (evoking the polonaise, krakowiak, and other Polish national dances) against the Russians' duple-meter and attractively lyrical music. In his *1812 Overture* (1880), Peter Tchaikovsky tracks Napoleon's fateful invasion of Russia with contrasting themes, including bits of "La Marseillaise" and "God Save the Tsar," the Russian imperial anthem. Several critics would liken Prokofiev's work to Nikolai Rimsky-Korsakov's opera *The Legend of the Invisible City of Kitezh* (1904), in which contrasting themes narrate a battle that unfolds before the curtain rises on act 3, scene 2. Yet these precedents involve themes that are developed—fragmented, layered, and otherwise transformed. Tchaikovsky, for instance, embeds fragmented bits of "La Marseillaise" in a symphonic passage that would have been at home in the development section of one of his symphonies. By contrast, Prokofiev composed short cues representing protagonists and antagonists that, when juxtaposed by Eisenstein in the cutting room, tracked the progress of the Battle on Ice without any intervening transitions or other development, like black-and-white contrasts realized musically. "Cavalry Attack," a rollicking, major-key galop, for instance, signals the Russians' upper hand. Cues that recycle music from the earlier Pskov sequence and the German psalm singing are heard when the Teutonic Knights are in the lead (much of this music is additionally the product of the recording studio; the psalm singing heard in the battle, for example, was recorded separately and overlaid on instrumental cues).[9] When Nevsky's troops finally chase the Teutonic Knights to their deaths on Lake Chudskoe, we once again hear "Cavalry Attack." Thus do Prokofiev and Eisenstein structure a battle that takes up nearly a third of the film. Bordwell's description of "exaggerated simplicity" is also appropriate here.

SOUNDING RUSSIAN

At the end of 1938, Eisenstein wrote a short text to accompany his recently completed film, devoted to the "great national struggle of the Russian people against aggression," as he described it. Predictably, he likened the Teutonic Knights' belligerence to present-day fascist aggression, and the national might of Alexander's forces to the strength of Stalin's Soviet Union, the "most wonderful country in the world." "My subject is patriotism," he asserted, a phrase "constantly in my mind and in the minds of our entire collective, during the shooting, the sound recordings and the montage."[10] Here Eisenstein engaged in a wise bit of politicking, trumpeting his successful realization of the state objectives we observed in chapter 1, namely to cultivate patriotism and national identity.

If we trust Eisenstein that patriotism was also his collaborators' subject, we might wonder how exactly a composer realizes such a goal. Patriotic music might call to mind anthems and military marches, as it seems to have done for Prokofiev when he began to set to music the second of Lugovskoi's three song texts, "Arise, Ye Russian People," the first phrase of which is in example 3.4. The result was a march that plays while the citizens of Novgorod come together and assemble for battle (35:05). Its opening eight measures

EXAMPLE 3.4 *Alexander Nevsky*, "Arise, Ye Russian People," mm. 1–8.

SERGEI PROKOFIEV'S *ALEXANDER NEVSKY*

feature an arch-shaped figure repeated twice (measures 1–4) followed by a second figure heard once (measures 5–8). Both figures contain no complex rhythms and only five distinct pitches, a deliberate simplicity meant to make the music immediately memorable. Repetition enhanced this goal; in the initial two-minute assembly sequence, for instance, the audience hears these two opening figures no fewer than five times. As listeners tapped their feet to the march's strong, foursquare pulse, mentally following a melody that was immediately familiar, they enacted the type of group affiliation that is the basis of patriotism.

It took far more, however, to give that sense of affiliation a specifically Russian identity. A key moment comes in the march's contrasting middle section, which features a hymn-like major-key tune intoned by alternating groups of men's and women's voices (36:07). When the composer Mikhail Cheremukhin heard this music in 1938, he likened it to the "restrained grandeur" of the choruses in Alexander Borodin's 1887 opera *Prince Igor*.[11] He most likely was thinking of the middle section of the opera's opening chorus, which, with its gently pulsing string texture and alternating male and female voices, does sound a great deal like the middle section of Prokofiev's "Arise." The comparison was significant; Borodin's opera was a classic of the Russian nationalist school that emerged in the later nineteenth century, and, by linking it to Prokofiev's music, Cheremukhin implied that his colleague had achieved something similarly nationally marked.

But why should Cheremukhin have thought of *Prince Igor* in particular? *Prince Igor* was thematically similar, to be sure—the opening chorus praises Igor, a prince who prepares to defend his homeland from foreign occupiers—but we could easily find analogous musical features in choruses by Giuseppe Verdi, Richard Wagner, and other nineteenth-century operatic composers. Most likely, other moments in the score primed Cheremukhin's reaction. For example, during the Battle on Ice, a group of Russian minstrels (known as *skomorokhi*) fires up the troops, one of the few times Prokofiev's music has an on-screen source in the film (figure 3.2 [1:10:36]). In the editing room, Eisenstein decided to intercut the very same musical sequence in the final Pskov sequence, when Alexander returns victoriously to the liberated city (1:46:05). This second iteration is more striking, as the minstrels' tune is echoed by an off-screen orchestral version, one that would strike those versed in late nineteenth-century Russian music

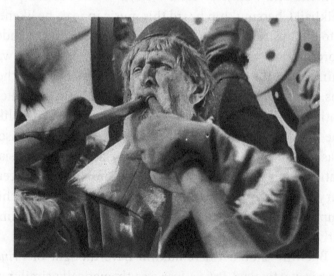

FIGURE 3.2 *Alexander Nevsky*, Minstrels (*skomorokhi*) playing during the Battle on Ice.

as uncannily familiar. Here Prokofiev's music is a dead ringer for the minstrel music that Rimsky-Korsakov composed for his opera *The Snow Maiden* (1880–81, rev. 1894–95). In both Rimsky-Korsakov's opera (example 3.5) and Prokofiev's film score (example 3.6), a winding, repetitive line weaves above the steady plucking of pizzicato

EXAMPLE 3.5   Nikolai Rimsky-Korsakov, *The Snow Maiden*, act 3, excerpt from the minstrels' music.

EXAMPLE 3.6 *Alexander Nevsky*, minstrels' music (orchestral version).

strings. Unlike the middle section of "Arise, Ye Russian People," Prokofiev's reference here is blatant, and it happens to be to another Russian nationalist classic. In fact, the *Nevsky* score is littered with such brief references, ones that surely predisposed Cheremukhin to think of Borodin rather than Verdi, even when there is only stylistic allusion rather than outright reference. In other words, to imbue the thirteenth century with a sense of Russian patriotism, Prokofiev turned to pieces that were already nationally marked for Russian listeners. These were the works of the so-called *Moguchaia Kuchka*, or "mighty little group," the oxymoronic name given to five nineteenth-century Russian composers—Borodin, Rimsky-Korsakov, Mily Balakirev, Cesar Cui, and Modest Musorgsky—who sought a school of composition distinct from that of Western Europe. Their music was propped up by folk song and an array of musical devices that, thanks to the Kuchka's prolific output and that of several younger generations of imitators, ended up sounding "Russian" to audiences by virtue of sheer quantity rather than any intrinsic quality.[12]

Prokofiev packed the *Nevsky* score's other vocal numbers with specific references as well. After the film's opening sequence, Alexander fishes with a group of men who sing about his victory over the Swedes ("Song about Alexander Nevsky"). Their calm melody unfolds under a striking, stratospherically high sustained pitch held by the violins for the first third of the song (3:47). This feature, on the one hand, is another of Prokofiev's stasis-inducing techniques, one that slows the audiovisual rhythm before the song's more active middle section (4:44), where strong accents in Prokofiev's music suggest the mechanical actions of onscreen boatbuilding. On the other hand, this sustained pitch figured, perhaps not surprisingly, into a number of prominent kuchkist works. The most famous is Borodin's musical portrait *In the Steppes of Central Asia* (1880), in which the composer used the high-pitched shimmer of sustained violins to evoke a distant horizon on the "boundless steppe," as he explained in a program note.[13] Borodin was, in fact, imitating Balakirev, who had used the same technique in the *Overture on the Themes of Three Russian Songs* (1858), a concert work in which the sustained pitch floats above a folk-like melody played on flutes and clarinets.

Likewise, moments of the lament that is sung following the Battle on Ice by a single mezzo-soprano voice ("The Field of the Dead") evoke Rimsky-Korsakov's opera *Sadko* (1895–96), specifically the lament in tableau 7. The melodic contours are similar, and, for those familiar with such things, both fluctuate between a minor key area and its relative major. Kuchkist composers were convinced this harmonic feature followed from Russian folk music, a conviction short on truth but ripe for nationalist development in their music. Some of Prokofiev's critics detected yet another reference in the lament's orchestral introduction, this one again to *Prince Igor*. At the opening of act 4 of the opera, Yaroslavna, Borodin's lead female character, mourns for her lost husband in an extended lament, one of the opera's most popular arias. Prokofiev uses a shimmering tremolo string texture—evoking the same in Borodin—with the melody doubled in octaves, Prokofiev's muted, Borodin's *sul ponticello* (placing the bow close to the bridge, yielding a thinner tone). Both have repeated rhythmic figures (a quarter note followed by two eighth notes) and similar melodic contours that alternate stepwise motion with minor thirds.

These and other references are fleeting yet highly suggestive. By calling to mind the work of Borodin and other kuchkist composers, Prokofiev forged an interpretive space tilted toward the national. Such a space predisposed an initiated listener to hear other parts of Prokofiev's score as intrinsically Russian and, when paired with image, to map Russian identity onto the thirteenth century, long before nationality even existed as a concept. Prokofiev's efforts paid off, especially among Soviet critics, and we will examine their reactions more fully in the following chapter.

Yet Prokofiev offered something for all listeners. Even those not fluent in the Russian classics responded to his military marches, hymn-like odes, and other patriotic gestures. In both film score and cantata, maximal stylistic contrasts—Russian lyricism versus German cacophony or stasis versus rhythmic drive—both propel the music forward and delineate a large-scale musical form not dependent on melodic or harmonic development. Finally, the atypical prominence of Prokofiev's music in the film, particularly in the many long sequences without dialogue, drew audiences into a story far removed in time from their own experience. In other words, as images of the thirteenth century flashed on the screen, cinemagoers' ears remained in familiar, nineteenth-century territory at key moments; as the composer Lev Shvarts later argued, it was Prokofiev's music more than anything that carried the audience "into the depths of the centuries." [14]

Prokofiev was presumably satisfied with the result, a film in which music is hardly handmaiden to image. He had, in essence, answered the question he had posed to himself almost a decade earlier when he wondered if it was "possible to write simple music that is completely accessible to the masses" without turning out trivial or insignificant works.[15] Viewed broadly, *Nevsky*'s accessibility was but one milestone on an extended exploration of the Great Divide we noted in chapter 1. Far more unique in the context of Prokofiev's career was his play with the nineteenth-century nationalist classics in *Nevsky*. The score's density of references and stylistic allusions might suggest a capitulation to Socialist Realist doctrine, the remit of which by the end of the 1930s narrowed ever more on nineteenth-century models. Yet Prokofiev's choices can be explained more convincingly as a response to *Alexander Nevsky*'s overall style and aims. What are Prokofiev's references to the Russian classics and his calculated accessibility if not efforts to stir up a nationally inflected patriotism among wide and diverse audiences? Yet these very features eased Prokofiev's music for *Nevsky* into the Socialist Realist canon, where it both overdetermined the reception of his later works—critics often heard kuchkist references where there were none—and served as a model for other composers. That is to say, Socialist Realism shaped *Nevsky* only indirectly, yet the film score and cantata played an outsized role in narrowing the doctrine's scope, a process that we will explore in the following chapter.

SCREEN TO STAGE, PART 1

By 1938 Prokofiev had long been a habitual repackager of his own music. The impulse was both pragmatic and careerist. For example, when Serge Diaghilev turned up his nose at *Ala and Lolli*, the first ballet offered to him by a young and green Prokofiev, the composer licked his wounds by refashioning the music as the *Scythian Suite* (1915), a successful concert work whose program loosely followed the failed ballet's scenario. Other such secondary works soon followed, even if the parent work was successful. For instance, even though Parisian audiences received the ballet *Chout* with enthusiasm, Prokofiev still chose to derive a concert suite (op. 21bis) from its music. In this fashion, Prokofiev got more mileage out of his efforts by transforming large and costly (and therefore risky and rarely performed) multimedia works into compact and easily programmable instrumental suites. The suites' publication augmented Prokofiev's bank account and ensured his music was not confined to the limited audiences of contemporary opera and ballet. During the past eighty years, for example, few have seen *Romeo and Juliet* staged, but, repackaged as suites (opp. 64bis, 64ter, and 101), the music became common and popular fare in concert seasons across the globe. Likewise, the *Lieutenant Kijé* Suite (1934) remains one of Prokofiev's most beloved pieces, while the film for which he composed the music is all but forgotten.

Little surprise, then, that we have a *Nevsky* concert work. But its genre—a cantata—stands out after a steady stream of suites, ten in all by 1938. Although the cantata originated as a narrative, sacred vocal-instrumental genre in the seventeenth century, the designation had come to refer to a broad range of medium-length works for orchestra and voices by the early twentieth. Arnold Schoenberg, for example, penned an entirely secular example (*Gurrelieder*, 1900–3/1910–11), Béla Bartók a folk-infused drama (*Cantata profana*, 1930), and Anton

Webern even introduced serial writing in his two cantatas (1939 and 1943). In the Soviet sphere, the cantata was a gift to ideologues bent on clear musical content, as the genre's text and overall narrative circumvented the subjectivity of instrumental works. And what better way to deliver a rousing political message than the combined forces of orchestra and choir, which might number over one hundred? Like many of his Soviet colleagues, Prokofiev jumped on the cantata bandwagon in the late 1930s, composing the *Cantata for the Twentieth Anniversary of October* (1937), a grandiose telling of the 1917 Revolution, and, following his work on *Nevsky*, *Zdravitsa* ("Hail to Stalin," 1939), a gift to Stalin on his sixtieth birthday. Given *Nevsky*'s broad choruses and bombastic tone, the cantata was an obvious choice for the form of this particular concert reworking.

Creating the *Nevsky* Cantata was no small task, however.[16] Although the film score's three large vocal numbers transferred to the cantata easily (becoming movements 2, 4, and 6; see table 3.1), many of the musical cues—especially those for the Battle on Ice—were far too short to stand alone. Movement 5 of the cantata, the "Battle on Ice," for example, is a patchwork of cues stitched together, often with newly composed passages added to smooth out the transitions. Orchestration was also a challenge; Prokofiev composed the *Nevsky* film score with a small studio orchestra in mind, likely a group of fewer than forty musicians. The studio microphone had also dictated many of his orchestration choices. He scored the music that accompanies Nevsky's duel with the Grand Master during the Battle on Ice primarily for brass and winds, for example,

TABLE 3.1   The *Alexander Nevsky* Cantata, op. 78.

1. Russia under the Mongolian Yoke
2. Song about Alexander Nevsky
3. The Crusaders in Pskov
4. Arise, Ye Russian People
5. The Battle on Ice
6. The Field of the Dead
7. Alexander's Entry into Pskov

a choice that at least one critic assumed was to make the music sound "metallic." [17] But Prokofiev knew that strings and percussion transferred poorly to tape, likely also the reason why he opted to use the dull thud of a box found in a Mosfilm storeroom rather than the sharp attack of a snare drum.[18]

Through stitching, recomposing, and re-orchestrating, Prokofiev ended up with a seven-movement work that follows the film's plot. Many critics doubted that such a cantata would form any kind of satisfying whole, as we will see. But consider how the Soviet musicologist Israel Nestyev, whose work we first noted in chapter 1, described the cantata's overall structure. That structure, he argued,

> has certain features of the sonata form. The first four movements represent the introduction and exposition of the main themes, and the fifth, in which the contrasting themes are contraposed and combined contrapuntally, is in the nature of a development section. These are followed by a lyrico-dramatic intermezzo (the sixth movement). The last movement, in which

the principal themes of the second and fourth movements are restated, serves as a recapitulation.[19]

Those familiar with the specifics of sonata form might find Nestyev's analysis forced, if not fanciful. Yet Nestyev was onto something, particularly how the music's stark contrasts yielded something of a narrative in sounds. Even if unfamiliar with Eisenstein's film, a listener could easily perceive a story of crisis, struggle, and victory. To be sure, neither Prokofiev himself nor Soviet music broadly had a monopoly on the trope of struggle-to-victory, which had loomed over European music since Beethoven immortalized it (think of the Fifth and Ninth Symphonies). It was nevertheless common in Soviet musical works of the 1930s; consider how Dmitri Shostakovich described his Fifth Symphony in 1937: "At the center of the work's conception I envisioned ... a man in all his suffering.... The symphony's finale resolves the tense and tragic moments of the preceding movements in a joyous, optimistic fashion."[20] Change man to nation, and you have the narrative of Prokofiev's cantata.

When the *Nevsky* Cantata premiered in Moscow on May 17, 1939, Europe stood on the precipice of war. In theaters, viewers heard Prokofiev's music in the context of a film created to buttress specific aims of the Soviet state. In concert halls, the music suggested a more general narrative of struggle and victory, one told through dramatic musical contrasts and abundant "visuality." As the works reached increasingly diverse audiences abroad, war shaped the ways in which they understood the images and sounds they saw and heard. It is to exploring this reception that we now turn.

CHAPTER 4

NEVSKY GOES TO WAR

O N THE EVENING OF November 28, 1938, a car spirited the writer and Party member Vsevolod Vishnevsky to Vasilevsky Street in northwest Moscow. He hurried through the entrance of building number 13 and into the viewing hall of the House of Cinema, a newly formed club for members of the Committee on Cinematography Affairs. When the lights dimmed at nine o'clock and the projector came to life, the opening scenes of *Alexander Nevsky* flashed on the screen. Lacking a proper notebook, Vishnevsky began jotting notes on the reverse of his admission ticket. His serpentine scrawl perhaps records some nervousness, as he had been charged with delivering the first public commentary on the film. If that was the case, he betrayed no anxiety when taking the podium following Prince

Alexander's concluding exhortation. Vishnevsky held forth in a similarly stately tone, commending "the talented master of Soviet cinematography Sergei Eisenstein," who, together with his collaborators, had created "the wonderful, deeply patriotic, and national film *Alexander Nevsky*." Once he got started, his praise came in torrents. Eisenstein had returned to the fold, he argued, a development that owed much to Pavlenko's ideologically correct scenario. At the conclusion of his extemporaneous appraisal, he singled out Prokofiev for the "enormous" scale of his work.[1]

Vishnevsky set an important precedent. A prominent cultural figure with a squeaky-clean political résumé, he modeled the tone for reviews that followed the film's December 1 general release. The critic Nikolai Kruzhkov wrote, for example, that tickets to the film were almost impossible to find, so motivated were Moscow viewers to see a film that could be "counted among the outstanding works of Soviet cinematography."[2] It was no small detail that Kruzhkov wrote for *Pravda*, the official organ of the Communist Party and the country's most politically orthodox periodical. Eisenstein engaged a clipping service to keep track of dozens of similar reviews. Whether he studied them carefully remains unclear; if he did, he would have learned that the only sustained criticism came from historians incensed by the film's historical inaccuracies.[3]

Almost all reviews applauded the work of *Nevsky*'s composer, though few engaged with Prokofiev's accomplishment in any detail. Nevertheless, this attention both enhanced Prokofiev's career in the Soviet Union and prepared the way for a project already hinted at in an addendum to the contract he had signed with Mosfilm eight months earlier.[4]

It granted ownership of the film's music to Prokofiev, who envisioned a concert work based on the film's music before he had even put pen to manuscript paper; as we saw in the previous chapter, it eventually became a cantata, a seven-movement work for orchestra, choir, and mezzo-soprano.[5] Prokofiev signed and dated the completed manuscript for the cantata on February 7, 1939, and conducted the Moscow Philharmonic in its premiere on May 17, demonstrating the viability of his score as a concert work.[6] By the end of the year, the cantata—now catalogued as Prokofiev's seventy-eighth opus—crowned the final concert of the third *Dekada* (ten-day festival) of Soviet Music, a retrospective showing of Soviet musical accomplishments (that in fact ran for nearly a month).[7] By then, popular groups such as the Red Army Choir had already added excerpts from the cantata to their active repertories. Prokofiev arranged portions of the choruses for solo voice and piano (op. 78a) and considered working on a version for piano four hands. These reformulations and arrangements, coming so quickly on the heels of the film's premiere, complicated the reception of Prokofiev's music. What exactly was Prokofiev's *Alexander Nevsky*? Was it the music attached to Eisenstein's film, an ephemeral presence emanating from theater speakers, inaccessible to listeners beyond the theater itself? Or was it the *Nevsky* Cantata, op. 78, a piece performed in concert, made tangible as scores and recordings, and generally accorded all of the attention of an independent work?

These questions concern more than semantics. Audiences engaged with each version in different and often contradictory ways. Many wondered whether film music, however rearranged, could stand on its own, a question that often harbored musty nineteenth-century views concerning originality and highbrow art. At the same time, many Soviet music critics balked at the idea that Prokofiev's accomplishment was but one half of Eisenstein's film. Rather, it was op. 78: a positive model for the development of Soviet music writ large, one to be pored over by generations of younger Soviet musicians. For international audiences, the leap from screen to stage put distance between Prokofiev's music and the film's Soviet Russian nationalism (not to mention its communist ties). Americans, for example, first heard the cantata during the Second World War, a very different context than the *Nevsky* film's US premiere in 1939. Critics in the United States most often viewed the cantata through a lens of generalized optimism rather than national specificity; conspicuously absent from American discussions were Eisenstein's name and the film's official origins in state propaganda. It is a familiar fact that the *Nevsky* Cantata quickly became a repertory staple on both sides of the Atlantic. The less familiar process by which this came to be is the topic of this chapter.

SCREEN TO STAGE, PART 2

Accounts of the triumphant general release of *Alexander Nevsky* in Moscow on December 1, 1938, are many. Reporters claimed that long lines wove their way around the city center and all twenty opening-day showings at the Metropole Hotel's three theaters sold out during the early hours of the morning. At the city's other main theaters, would-be viewers who arrived too late tried to purchase advance tickets for showings later in the week. The following day a correspondent for the newspaper *Kino* breathlessly reported that forty-five thousand tickets had already been sold in the capital's seven main theaters.[8] For a Soviet public that had been fed a steady diet of announcements and tantalizing progress reports on the film since the summer, the premiere was a major event not to be missed.

Predestined, foretold, or otherwise, the success was singular: Eisenstein and his collaborators basked in the spotlight of popular acclaim, if not political favor. Even a report in the *New York Times* five days after the general release described "tremendous popular success" that portended the director's return to favor from "oblivion."[9] We also know, thanks to a cache of archival materials that includes fan letters to Eisenstein, that the film had an actual impact on everyday citizens in the USSR. David Brandenberger, a historian who has studied these materials extensively, concludes that "fundamental changes in the party hierarchy's patriotic sloganeering, epitomized by the grand historical vision of Eisenstein's *Aleksandr Nevskii*," had a "tangible effect on Soviet social *mentalité*." For example, viewers freely interchanged onscreen fantasy and geopolitical reality, discussing the contemporary Nazi threat with reference to the character and historical figure of Nevsky. Brandenberger also convincingly argues that the "widespread interest and enthusiasm" with which *Nevsky* was met confirmed the viability of historical films in general, setting the stage for later historical-biographical pictures like *Minin and Pozharsky* (1939) and *Suvorov* (1941).[10]

The success of *Alexander Nevsky* both impressed and disillusioned Prokofiev. Enjoying the post-premiere excitement, he and Eisenstein bandied about plans for a new (but ultimately unrealized) film about the Russian Civil War, *Periscope*.[11] Other directors courted him too, and he signed up for Vasily Pronin's *The Commandant of Bird Island*, a drama about the Soviet frontier guard's efforts against Japanese spies.[12] A month after *Nevsky's* premiere, it was Prokofiev's turn to go to the House of Cinema, where cinema luminaries fêted him for an entire evening (the event included an address by musicologist Viktor Tsukkerman and a concert of Prokofiev's music).[13] Heady enthusiasm fizzled out as the spring drew on, however. Pronin and his film fell off the radar; the composer Vano Muradeli signed up in Prokofiev's stead. By early summer 1939, even Eisenstein was out, the artistic love affair ended by a memo from Prokofiev: "I continue to consider cinema the most modern art, but precisely because of its novelty in our country we haven't learned to value its constituent parts and consider music to be some sort of appendage, unworthy of any particular attention."[14] Other projects had landed on Prokofiev's desk, to be sure, and experience taught him that work with Eisenstein could be all-consuming. He griped to his wife, for instance, that it would be impossible "to keep up with everything" if he continued work with the director.[15] Money was also a concern. The generous honorarium paid to Prokofiev for *Nevsky* followed from the film's unusually large budget, and the Mosfilm administration intimated that he would be paid, at best, half that amount for subsequent films.[16] Yet Prokofiev's complaint to Eisenstein—that music lacked *particular* attention—speaks more to reviewers such as Kruzhkov, who had granted the composer a single, crisp line in

Pravda ("Prokofiev's wonderful score is commendable"). For Prokofiev, formulaic praise was abundant; the critical spotlight was not.

The *Nevsky* Cantata proved far more gratifying on the latter count. Of particular importance were the two performances we have already noted (the May premiere and the concluding concert of the *dekada*), which drew the attention of music critics who had been silent on the film score.[17] The most assiduous of these was Israel Nestyev, whose commentary on the *Nevsky* Cantata's formal structure we noted in the previous chapter. At the premiere, the music's allusions to nineteenth-century Russian national music charmed him. Here was the "national-epic canvas of Glinka, Borodin, [and] Rimsky-Korsakov," he declared. He added that the second movement ("Song about Alexander Nevsky") would have sent Vladimir Stasov, the Kuchka's belligerent propagandist, "into ecstasy." He also implied that Prokofiev, the great cosmopolitan musician, had something to teach Soviet composers about genres they themselves had developed. "Arise, Ye Russian People," for example, brimmed with "national color, unlike the saccharine, conventional folk character of many of our mass songs."[18] Other critics echoed these sentiments following the *dekada* performance later in the year. The composer Lev Shvarts, for instance, highlighted the opening chorus's "calm, fresh theme presented and harmonized in the traditions of the composers of the 'Moguchaia Kuchka.'"[19] One S. Marich felt these qualities evinced a monumentality that made Prokofiev's cantata one of the first Soviet cantatas.[20] Prokofiev, along with Yuri Shaporin and Marian Koval, composers who had also contributed historically themed

FIGURE 4.1   Viktor Vasnetsov, *Epic Warriors* (*Bogatyri*, 1898).

cantatas to the *dekada* (*On Kulikovo Field* and *Emelian Pugachev*), were branded *bogatyri*, or epic warriors. Soviet audiences likely chuckled that Viktor Vasnetsov's familiar 1898 painting of three such *bogatyri* (figure 4.1) had been repurposed by artist Mikhail Aleksich to suggest the scale of the achievements of Prokofiev, Shaporin, and Koval (figure 4.2).

Yet Prokofiev was far more famous and also far more suspect than Shaporin or Koval, neither of whom had built a career in the West. As Stalin's Russia grew ever more closed, Western connections—let alone years abroad—were regarded with suspicion. Here Nestyev came to the rescue, insisting that Prokofiev had reawakened a nationalist voice that had hibernated during his cosmopolitan decades abroad. He reminded his readers that the influential critic Igor Glebov (the pen name of Boris Asafiev) had once likened Prokofiev's 1916 *Scythian Suite* to Borodin's classics,

FIGURE 4.2   Mikhail Aleksich's caricature of Prokofiev, Shaporin, and
Koval, made following the final concert of the 1939 *dekada*.
I. Nest'ev. *Zhizn' Sergeia Prokof'eva*, 2nd ed. (Moscow:
Kompozitor, 1973), 425.

which were "singular, mighty, invoking both the steppe's
expanse and wild spontaneity." That the same comparison
could be made with the *Nevsky* Cantata, Nestyev reasoned,
was evidence enough that Prokofiev had picked up where
he had left off twenty-three years ago, conveniently cordon-
ing off the years the composer had spent living outside of
Russia.[21] Shvarts was even more direct, arguing that *Nevsky*
was "a work remarkable not only for the depth of its musical thought but also for its evidence of the composer's serious artistic reform."[22] By evoking "reform"—*perestroika*
in Russian—Shvarts fitted Prokofiev into a stock plot pio-
neered by Dmitri Shostakovich, whose Fifth Symphony
evinced a similar *perestroika* following a notorious 1936
attack on the composer's modernist style in *Pravda*. The

composer Vano Muradeli found it "particularly gratifying that this is some kind of a new Prokofiev, not the composer of the dark and intricate Third and Fourth Symphonies—this is Prokofiev looking at art with the eyes of a true Soviet artist." [23]

Despite kuchkisms more than a half century old being the clear attraction, the same battalion of critics praised Prokofiev for his originality. Consider Nestyev's contradictory assertion that in the *Nevsky* Cantata the "melodic flexibility of Glinka and Borodin and the scenically precise imagery of Rimsky-Korsakov are developed," but, at the same time, they "never hinder the independence of the composer." [24] Marich liked the "bold, expressive means" that resulted from "artistic innovation," even though he was talking about the very kuchkisms that made for a "true historical flavor of an epoch far removed from our own." [25] Far from critical lapses, these assertions retrofitted nationalist film music with the high-art romantic values of the stage, in which originality, innovation, and influence on others were the measures of greatness. Indeed, the composer and bureaucrat Dmitri Kabalevsky—a frequent chronicler of composer *perestroiki*—advised his readers that they failed to realize "the great influence that *Alexander Nevsky* will inevitably have on the later growth of Soviet music." [26]

Why was Kabalevsky so confident? As we already noted, by the end of the 1930s, professional discussion in Soviet music circles increasingly valued identifiable, programmatic content and an audience-friendly style rooted in the Russian classics. The *Nevsky* Cantata had both in spades. Indeed, Prokofiev's cantata, thanks to its parent work, came prepackaged with a narrative that explained its content.

Marich, for example, applauded Prokofiev's "counterpoint, harmony, and instrumentation," which were deployed solely for the "expression of the work's lofty poetic idea."[27] Nestyev went further, arguing that the "abstract, contrived delusions" of Prokofiev's dissonant, complex music (i.e., the works he composed while living abroad) had found an appropriate application in conveying the invading knights' character, making their connection to "Europe's modern barbarians" viscerally apparent.[28] Justifying dissonance on narrative grounds was nothing new in the Socialist Realist lexicon (indeed, the theme of war presented many opportunities for such music, as Marina Frolova-Walker has shown).[29] At the same time, Nestyev betrayed some anxiety that Prokofiev's musical images derived from the middle-brow world of cinema. But history again came to the rescue:

> There are likely to be objections to *Alexander Nevsky*'s excessive visuality. It is, to be sure, a clear example of theatrical, programmatic-descriptive symphonism. But Prokofiev interweaves outwardly descriptive means ... with episodes of deep musical reflection (choruses, aria). Even in the most descriptive scenes (the Knights in Pskov and the Battle on Ice), Prokofiev relies on both the imitation of sounds (the horses' footfall, the soldiers' gait, the ringing of bells) and purely musical categories such as leitmotivs, as is the case with the best examples of classic battle music ([Franz Liszt's] *Battle of the Huns*, [Rimsky-Korsakov's] "Battle of Kerzhenets").[30]

Thus even Prokofiev's most cinematic moments could be rescued by invoking precedents in the art music tradition (Liszt's work is a symphonic poem, Rimsky-Korsakov's an entr'acte from the opera *Invisible City of Kitezh*). In a telling passage, Marian Koval griped that the cantata's "musical images are perceived only when paired with the film's visual associations," and he claimed that separating the two yielded something "less serious."[31] Yet Koval's own cantata, *Emelian Pugachev*, had paled next to Prokofiev's. Reading his comments through the lens of professional jealousy might suggest the extent to which his complaints in fact pointed to Prokofiev's accomplishments.

The public discourse of Nestyev and others paralleled that of the newly formed Stalin Prize Committee, charged with recognizing achievement in the Soviet arts and sciences with state awards, graded by first and second classes (a third was added later). In the first round, which recognized projects completed between 1934 and 1940, Eisenstein and two of *Alexander Nevsky*'s actors received awards. Prokofiev did not, leading some scholars to assume that his music had not been that highly regarded after all. Yet archival records reveal that the *Nevsky* Cantata was in fact a serious contender for the award. Committee members such as the pianist Alexander Goldenweiser argued that it was a wholly Soviet work, even if Prokofiev's earlier pieces had caused many to doubt if the composer was "in tune with our Soviet reality."[32] The composer Nikolai Miaskovsky maintained that if given a proper performance, the post-battle lament (which had become the sixth movement of the cantata) "would be a song to which Glinka would have signed his name. It is exceptional in depth, sincerity, and warmth of feeling."[33] However, Prokofiev's main detractor here was a powerful bureaucrat, Mikhail Khrapchenko. As Khrapchenko claimed in a memo to one of Stalin's advisors, "the suite 'Alexander Nevsky' is not an outstanding piece of music. It is based on music for the film *Alexander Nevsky* and has not gained any wide popularity." Branded a derivative work, the *Nevsky* Cantata was passed over for official recognition.[34]

NEVSKY *CROSSES THE OCEAN*

At nearly the same time, during the first half of 1941, the American photographer Margaret Bourke-White traveled through the Soviet Union, documenting various aspects of the country's industry and culture. Arriving in Moscow, she and her husband, Erskine Caldwell, called on Eisenstein at Mosfilm. The director treated the couple to an impromptu showing, one that Bourke-White led readers of her memoirs to believe was quite special: "[Eisenstein] got the reels out of a safe where they were stored away and gave Erskine and me a private showing. 'We think,' he commented sagely, 'that it will not be much longer before *Alexander Nevsky* will be shown in public cinema theaters again.'"[35] Bourke-White implies that *Nevsky* had been entombed since August 1939, when the Soviet Union brokered a nonaggression pact with Nazi Germany. There was evidence to support her story: already in September, readers of the *New York Times* learned that the "communazi" pact had made a taboo of anti-Nazi sentiment in the USSR, and propaganda films such as *Nevsky* had been quietly shelved.[36] Rumors circulated that two other Soviet films suffered a similar fate, *Professor Mamlok* (1938) and *The Oppenheim Family* (1939), both of which documented Nazi abuse of Jews. By the time Jay Leyda published his influential history of Soviet film in 1960, these anecdotes were lodged in the historical record.

Like many tales of Soviet censorship that blossomed at moments of strained US-USSR relations, *Alexander Nevsky*'s shelving (and supposed post-haste return to theaters following the Nazi invasion of 1941) is greatly exaggerated. Eisenstein collected dozens of clippings from Soviet newspapers that demonstrate *Nevsky* was alive and well in Soviet theaters after the nonaggression pact was signed.[37] In May 1940 an article even appeared in *Pravda*, that most official of public organs, boasting of the film's success in Estonia.[38] Moreover, as we have already seen, Eisenstein managed to net a Stalin Prize for *Nevsky* during the brokered peace of 1939–41. Yet rumors of top-down censorship proved compelling, as they supported international suspicions concerning the vagaries of government control of the arts in the Soviet Union. Audiences and critics had warmly received *Alexander Nevsky* following the US premiere on March 22, 1939, and the UK premiere a month later. The former was particularly hyped; President Roosevelt had a special showing at the White House, and, following the general premiere, special showings popped up on Broadway.[39] News of *Nevsky*'s mothballing must have been striking; for the international viewers who applauded the film during late spring and summer 1939, the imagined prohibition either confirmed that *Nevsky* was state propaganda (rather than the creative work of an internationally renowned director) or that great Soviet artists had fallen victim to state politics. Both explanations have always been popular ways of thinking about Soviet art, particularly among Anglophone audiences.

The *Nevsky* Cantata arrived in the United States under markedly different circumstances. Prokofiev first learned of a planned performance in late March 1942, nine months following the Nazi invasion of the USSR and well into the wartime evacuations that had spirited him away from Moscow to the south of Russia. A bureaucrat from the Soviet All-Union Society for Cultural Ties Abroad (usually known by its Russian acronym, VOKS) requested a program note to accompany a performance of the cantata the following month in New York. The invitation must have been enticing: VOKS was the main conduit of Soviet music to the West, and to date the cantata had received no international attention save for a single radio broadcast performance in England.[40] With his American audience in mind, Prokofiev began his note with some historical context, describing Nevsky's heroism in the face of German aggressors. He closed by evoking the contemporary struggle for "noble ideals and future peace," a battle that Prokofiev implied paralleled Nevsky's seven hundred years earlier (a translation of the complete program note is in the appendix to this book).[41]

Prokofiev couldn't resist a bit of spin, both for VOKS officials who promoted the cantata and its soon-to-be American consumers. Relating each movement to the visual sequence it originally accompanied, he concluded that the cantata retained a "certain element of visuality." Some musicians had condemned this quality, he admitted, but it had been a necessary concession to comprehensibility. Here was a retooled version of Prokofiev's long-standing suspicion of mass audiences. Passages that seemed to have an unmistakable visual analogue, such as the third movement's "clang of iron" and "cries of women and children," defined a populist style like a life vest buoying up an inexperienced listener in otherwise abstract waters. At the same time, Prokofiev insisted that he had "spent much more effort" on the cantata than on the film score, assuring his listeners that the cantata was not simply a film score without a film.[42] In other words, the populist and comprehensible cantata was hardly tossed off by the composer for a quick performance. It demanded the same kind of hard labor as that behind symphonies, operas, and other large-scale, "serious" undertakings. Thus Prokofiev preemptively countered suspicions that the cantata was a derivative work, for how could the cantata be a byproduct if it demanded more effort than its parent work?

However, another VOKS-sponsored work, Dmitri Shostakovich's Seventh Symphony (1941), preempted Prokofiev's in America's concert halls. Shostakovich's work came with a much more marketable back story, Shostakovich having composed the first two movements during the siege of Leningrad. Encouraged by a barrage of publicity and newspaper reports, American audiences perceived in the symphony a wordless narrative of war, one that conveyed the horrors of invasion and predicted the glories of victory. The viability of war-themed Soviet works having been demonstrated, Leopold Stokowski premiered the *Nevsky* Cantata the following season with the NBC Symphony Orchestra and Westminster Choir. Reviewing the March 7, 1943, performance at New York's Radio City Music Hall (simultaneously broadcast on WEAF) for the *New York Times*, Olin Downes wrote that Prokofiev demonstrated that "a work of art can have not only historical but prophetic associations." He also praised the "well-made score," a count on which Paul Bowles agreed in the *New York Herald Tribune*: "It is hard to understand the excitement caused by the music of Shostakovich here and in the Soviet Union, when Prokofieff is there making such scores as this." [43] At least in the ears of these two critics, Prokofiev could also play wartime prophet, and do so far better than Shostakovich.

Prokofiev had long impressed Downes, a critic who for nearly two decades had been a powerful arbiter of American musical culture. While Prokofiev apologized for the occasional concession to accessibility, Downes embraced it. As he told a radio audience in 1945, Prokofiev's music was "stripped of every superfluity or ornamentation, concise but rich in ideas—music of an artist who is not a politician nor a propagandist nor a self-elected high priest, but just an artist, ripened by suffering and experience and creating for a better day." In short, Prokofiev was the antithesis of the art-for-art's-sake stance defended by many modern composers, particularly Downes's *bête noire*, Igor Stravinsky. Stravinsky "abjured his musical nationalism" in favor of an "architectural art," Downes argued, a crime tantamount to the "escapism" of ignoring totalitarian threat. "There was the fervent hope that by ignoring evil that stared us in the face, we might escape the necessity of heroic action and sacrifice," he wrote, "and it seems very clear to me that this same futile escapism has been all too strong an element in modern music." [44]

Downes presumably felt vindicated on April 3, 1945, when Eugene Ormandy led the Philadelphia Orchestra, the Westminster Choir, and the mezzo-soprano Rosalind Nadell in the Carnegie Hall premiere of the *Nevsky* Cantata. Relating the audience's ecstatic approval to his readers, Downes insisted that "the composers today of direct and unadorned statement are few, and still fewer have the background, technical resource and dramatic spirit of Prokofieff to carry out similar intentions." The music was perhaps not Prokofiev's most original, he added, but

> its sincerity and inspiration are unmistakable, and it swept the audience from its feet.... There are, no doubt, composers of not half the stature of Prokofieff, who might sniff, albeit enviously, at such broad brushstrokes and unashamed appeal to patriotism as this. They would do well to come anywhere near it for inspiration and articulateness.[45]

One who did sniff was the oft-dyspeptic composer Arthur Berger, who complained generally about the popularity of Soviet works with American audiences. "Some undertakings," he carped, "are easily eclipsed by inferior ones which survive through an accidental or contrived conspiracy with our dominant international sympathies or conceptual concerns of the moment."[46] Although serving different ends, Berger's and Downes's assertions speak to the same truism, that wartime had afforded unprecedented opportunities for works like the *Nevsky* Cantata. Berger implies that Prokofiev's work would never have gained a foothold during peacetime, when works perceived as being "above politics"—the transcendent classics and objective modernist exercises—assured the high-art status of symphonic institutions.

Downes was not alone in his adulation, however. At the same concert was the critic Donald Fuller, who dashed off the following for the influential specialist journal *Modern Music*:

> [Prokofiev] had not attempted a work on a really heroic scale since the *Scythian Suite*, which many wish had served as more

of a point of departure for his whole development. The gray, poignant landscape of the opening is huge and exciting and its icy tone penetrates much of the cantata. There is a tautness in the chorus's folksong style which never relaxes into the easy, distended sentiment rarely avoided in such writing for large groups. Nor are there the usual unpleasantly calculated climaxes. Only after one has been swept to the high points is there time to realize how irresistibly one was taken there. The section depicting the battle on the ice has an especial force. The orchestration is admirable for its superb sound, but above all for its delineation of a richly allusive atmosphere, as fine in its way as Stravinsky's very different evocation in the *Symphonie des Psaumes* [*sic*].[47]

Fuller compliments the work entirely on its own terms; the pacing he so especially enjoyed is understood with no reference to the film score. Likewise, his oblique mention of the work's visuality serves—*pace* Downes—as a pivot to Stravinsky's *Symphony of Psalms*, a work many regarded as the antithesis of populist or nationalist music. In Fuller's account, there is no mention of *Nevsky*'s back story, reducing the narrative that drives the work to unspecific "allusion." Most remarkably, Fuller connects Prokofiev's early and recent work in the same manner as Nestyev, tacitly dismissing Prokofiev's long international career. Yet here, as with Downes, the praise is for heroic tone rather than national style. Far more blunt on these counts was Paul Bowles, who wrote in the *New York Herald Tribune* that

if the work in its new form inevitably suggests the visual images it was originally intended to accompany, it thereby becomes no less impressive as a piece of atmospheric music; indeed, there is little doubt that this cantata will be fresh, vigorous and inspiring long after the film has faded from the memory of all but the archivists.[48]

In the critical discourse, *Nevsky* had lurched away from its original context, even the expurgated and apologetic frame Prokofiev himself had provided for American audiences.

Arguably the seminal moment in the *Nevsky* Cantata's ascent to international prominence was the first commercial recording, made by Ormandy with the Philadelphia Orchestra about a month after the Carnegie Hall performance. By late 1945, the Columbia Masterworks series shuttled Prokofiev's work around the country on five 78-rpm discs, a recording immediately incorporated into playlists of radio stations.[49] The recording was a crucial addition to Prokofiev's relatively meager showing in record catalogues; besides early works such as the Classical Symphony, the Violin Concertos, and the composer's own recording of the Third Piano Concerto, listeners without access to major concert halls knew little of his music. Columbia reissued the recording on LP in 1949, complete with cover art by the then twenty-one-year-old Andy Warhol (figure 4.3). Now more than seven decades old, the recording is still breathtaking in its virtuosity and immediacy. Listeners used to more recent recordings will find the tempos brisk and the string and brass playing to have an exceptionally bristling edge. The directness impressed: Mark Schubert, writing in the *New York Times*, noted the cantata's "loud noises" and patriotism, but the former was "impressive" and the latter had "passion."[50] Likewise, the critic Irving Kolodin seems to have been underwhelmed by the score (he relates that

FIGURE 4.3   Jacket cover of Columbia ML 4247 (1949) with drawing by
Andy Warhol.

a colleague branded it "public-square music") but wowed by Ormandy's delivery, which was "impressively vigorous" and "muscular," the entire project a testament to Columbia's achievements in recording.[51]

Officials at VOKS presumably thought *Nevsky* had been a coup, insofar as it fulfilled their charge to promote Soviet cultural achievements abroad. TASS, the Soviet news agency, picked up excerpts of reviews of the 1945 Ormandy performance and transmitted them back to Moscow for inclusion in Soviet newspapers.[52] VOKS representatives recognized Prokofiev's popularity in the United States and dispatched a copy of the score for the *Nevsky* Cantata to Helen Black, the head of Am-Rus Music, a New York–based firm that maintained a library of Soviet music for hire and publication. Black immediately arranged for Leeds Music to publish the score, which was out in stores by the end of 1945 (figure 4.4).[53] VOKS and Am-Rus/Leeds were not alone in capitalizing on *Nevsky*'s popularity. The Sam Fox publishing company had beaten them to the punch with an unauthorized arrangement of "Arise, Ye Russian People" for chorus and piano. Sold under the title "Fight for Freedom," it offered would-be performers a banal ode to universal strife in place of Lugovskoi's text: "Arise, brave people, ev'rywhere, for freedom's cause with heart and hand, arise, strong people all who care for liberty in ev'ry land." Black complained to Moscow about the transgression, hoping to hear Prokofiev's opinion on the matter. His response does not survive.[54]

ON THE PRECIPICE OF THE COLD WAR

As Columbia's first pressings of the new recording went into circulation, the *Nevsky* Cantata, performed by the New York Philharmonic led by Stokowski (with the famed Jennie Tourel singing the sixth-movement solo) filled the cavernous expanses of Madison Square Garden on December 18, 1945. The occasion, billed as "USA-USSR: Welding the Peace" and sponsored by the Greater New York Committee of the American Society for Russian Relief, also featured a battery of short speeches that ranged from Mayor Fiorello LaGuardia's appeals for "understanding" and "friendship"

FIGURE 4.4   Cover page of the first American edition of the *Nevsky* Cantata.
*Serge Prokofieff, Alexander Nevsky, Cantata for Chorus and
Orchestra* (New York: Leeds, 1945).

to calls for active student exchanges with the Soviet Union.[55] Downes, asked to introduce the musical attraction, did not shy away from his agenda. "[The Soviets] did not prattle of 'art for art's sake,'" he bellowed; "it was art for humanity's sake."[56] Downes's comments spilled over into a *New York Times* article published five days later, in which he lectured that although "80 per cent of the blood shed by all the nations that fought Germany in the second World War was Russia's," the country's artists "created fully 80 per cent, if not more, of the important music produced in the whole western world during the period of the conflict." He credited this accomplishment to the communicative power of national art and the Soviet government's beneficent attitude toward its artists. "Circumstances have shown that in Russia music is considered an indispensable part of living," he added, "and not a matter of after-dinner entertainment or a civilization's window dressing."[57] Prokofiev learned about the Stokowski performance through VOKS, prompting him to cable the conductor the following:

> Sending you and all performers of "Alexander Nevsky" my sincerest and friendliest greetings. Ardently wishing this composition as well as the music of my Soviet and American colleagues may strengthen mutual spiritual understanding and cultural ties between our great peoples.[58]

Shortly thereafter, Prokofiev received a letter from his old friend Dukelsky. "'Alexander Nevsky' is a tremendous success here," he reported, "and has been superbly recorded, as you undoubtedly know. The Cantata version is ten times more impressive than the film music." The

cantata, he added, showed "a tendency to become repertory staple." [59]

The *Nevsky* Cantata had managed what few Soviet
works did. It had crossed the Atlantic, received multiple
performances by major orchestras, earned accolades from
major critics, and been issued by a major record label.
(Indeed, plans were underway in 1946 to ship copies of
Ormandy's recording to the USSR, where no recording
yet existed.) Timing was everything: a work so direct in
its Russian theme and style would hardly have been so
welcome before 1941 or after 1945, when relations between
the Soviet Union and United States were less amica-
ble. But the war and the rhetoric of critics like Downes
momentarily upset highbrow and middlebrow categories,
opening a place for the work. As the world's superpow-
ers moved from wartime alliance toward postwar antag-
onism, the cantata was firmly ensconced in Soviet and
Western repertories.

CHAPTER 5

FROM HOT WAR
TO COLD WAR

I N LATE 1949, music lovers in New York and London discovered a new offering in music shops: a piano-vocal
score of the *Alexander Nevsky* Cantata published simultaneously by Leeds (in the United States) and Boosey and
Hawkes (in England). Suitably compact at eighty-six pages
in length and with texts in both Russian and English
translation, it facilitated rehearsals for choral groups per-
forming the work. It also testified to the cantata's continued popularity, particularly with Anglophone audiences.
New recordings of op. 78 appeared, and critics continued discussing the work, albeit in ways that increasingly
unmoored Prokofiev's music from its Soviet context.
The same could not be said of the film *Alexander Nevsky*.
Showings in the West plummeted, the film's barefaced

Russian patriotism now unpalatable as Cold War tensions escalated. Absent from theaters and the popular imagination, *Nevsky* increasingly became a specialist interest, a picture pored over by film scholars attracted by Eisenstein's voluminous theoretical writings. Here, Prokofiev's music figured into discussions concerned more with audiovisual form than agitprop content. In the Soviet Union, the situation was, of course, quite different. Officials accorded both film and cantata "classic" status, the former nourishing a collective unity forged in the cauldron of war and the latter serving as a conservative reference point as Khrushchev's "Thaw" brought unpredictable changes to Soviet musical circles.

Rhetoric situated Prokofiev's music in these different contexts. In the Soviet Union, for instance, bureaucratic fiat and quasi-scholarly dogmatizing determined whether lovers of Prokofiev's cantata heard the work or not. Across the Atlantic, commentators were at pains to justify the popularity of a concert work derived from a film that buttressed what had come to be regarded as one of the twentieth century's most repressive regimes. To untangle these creative and scholarly histories is to understand something of musical values. Questions of craft, contemporaneity, timelessness, simplicity, and technical sophistication can be both reflective and prescriptive, testifying to the ways in which diverse listeners experienced or *should* experience Prokofiev's music during the second half of the twentieth century. In other words, how did listeners, writers, and bureaucrats alike prolong, channel, or appropriate the immediate and often visceral popularity of *Alexander Nevsky*'s music we traced in the last chapter?

RUSSKAIA KLASSIKA, SOVETSKAIA KLASSIKA

Israel Nestyev, who first lauded the *Nevsky* Cantata back in 1939, had by the end of the war firmly grabbed hold of the coattails of its famous composer. In 1945 he successfully defended a doctoral dissertation on Prokofiev and convinced the New York publisher Alfred A. Knopf to publish his study in English, a coup that says something about Prokofiev's popularity in the West.[1] If anything, Nestyev's esteem for the *Nevsky* Cantata had grown. It still marked Prokofiev's reconnection with a national language that extended back to Mikhail Glinka, but now it also colored Prokofiev's more recent compositions. A "Borodin" line extended, Nestyev argued, from the *Nevsky* Cantata through the opera *War and Peace* (first version, 1941–43) to the Fifth Symphony (1944).[2] Although *Nevsky*'s overt kuchkist allusions and references are absent from the latter two works, Nestyev nonetheless insisted that the lush symphonic style of all three should be heard with the conspicuous nationalism of the first ringing in the ears. His was a smart move concerning the Fifth Symphony, which, unlike *Nevsky* and *War and Peace*, was textless and without a program. By insisting on its kinship with *Nevsky*, Nestyev imparted the requisite concreteness and *narodnost* that admitted the work to the Socialist Realist canon. (By contrast, the American composer and critic Virgil Thomson expressed surprise at how little seemed quintessentially Russian in Prokofiev's Fifth.)[3]

Everything changed in January 1948. It was then that the Central Committee of the Communist Party of the Soviet Union, having already issued new ideological standards for literature and cinema, turned its attention to music. A resolution, promulgated by the notorious bureaucrat Andrei Zhdanov, charged Prokofiev and other leading composers with perpetuating a "formalist and anti-people school," one that delighted in "atonalism, dissonance, and disharmony," which were "alleged to be signs of 'progress' and 'innovation.'"[4] Nestyev's adulation makes for absurd reading in this context. Zhdanov, for example, accused Prokofiev of ignoring Russian traditions and thus compromising the accessibility of his music to the masses. Even more ludicrous was an accusation that emerged during subsequent discussion of the resolution that Prokofiev was someone who "still believes in 'innovation for innovation's sake,' [who] has an artistic snobbishness, a false fear of being commonplace or ordinary."[5] Intended to assert strong bureaucratic control of Soviet music as the Cold War escalated, the resolution amounted to an unprecedented takedown of the vanguard of Soviet music, one from which Prokofiev never fully recovered. The resolution demanded that composers write music with identifiable content in an accessible, anti-modernist style modeled on the nineteenth-century classics—Socialist Realism, in other words—a regressive position intended to generate ever more stark ideological boundaries with the West. (Nestyev, an indirect victim of the resolution, lost his day job in the state radio administration and began writing about Tchaikovsky's music, a far safer topic after 1948. Perhaps to save his own skin, he also accused Prokofiev of formalist distortions in this Sixth Symphony, a work he had praised as a "classic" only days earlier in the composer's presence; Prokofiev never forgave Nestyev for his betrayal.)[6]

While Prokofiev's concert and stage works languished under a cloud of suspicion, Eisenstein's film was canonized. As Nina Tumarkin and other historians have documented, Prince Alexander had been subsumed into a sacred image of war, Stalin himself even proffering the prince as an example of wartime valor as Nazi troops threatened Moscow. Special mobile projection units had shown excerpts from the Battle on Ice at the front lines, and Stalin instituted the "Order of Alexander Nevsky," a state award for wartime heroism (the image on the medal resembled Nikolai Cherkasov). A sense of national unity coalesced around these and other sounds and images, one that Soviet power had never successfully managed to bring about during peacetime. Collective loss and victory became, in Tumarkin's words, a "sustaining myth" that would be perpetuated for decades by a "failing political system" seeking legitimacy.[7] *Alexander Nevsky* was thus unassailable; by the end of the decade critics and bureaucrats alike referred to the film as a classic. And so too, in 1948, did Prokofiev's film score retain its status as a classic while his other works (including the *Nevsky* Cantata) vanished from concert halls.[8] In a June 1948 essay, Lev Shvarts cautiously acknowledged the years Prokofiev had spent "soak[ing] up the urban culture of the contemporary West," but he boasted that the *Nevsky* film score was one of the best "examples of choral and symphonic style, one entirely supported by the remarkable traditions of Russian kuchkism." "His chorus 'Arise, Ye Russian People,'" Shvarts gushed, "may rightfully take a place alongside the best classical works of this genre."[9] Even Tikhon Khrennikov, one of Prokofiev's most hostile critics during the 1948 affair, begrudgingly acknowledged the film score's quality and political correctness.[10]

And then, in what Richard Taruskin has called "a coincidence no novelist would dare contrive," Prokofiev died of a cerebral hemorrhage on March 5, 1953, just as news of Stalin's own death spread rapid-fire through the USSR.[11] By the time Nikita Khrushchev denounced Stalin's excesses in his 1956 "Secret Speech," Prokofiev was well on his way to posthumous canonization as a Soviet classic. Although this turn of fortune was in part a simple rolling back of Stalin-era ideological excesses, there was a distinctly pragmatic element as well. As the comparatively open Khrushchev years fostered greater stylistic diversity in music composition, Soviet commentators remarked increasingly on Prokofiev's international renown and his post-1920s resistance to Western modernist trends such as neoclassicism and dodecaphony. He thus functioned as stable reference point for conservative bureaucrats as the cultural landscape around them was changing rapidly, a composer who was, unlike Shostakovich, deceased and therefore unchanging. In death, Prokofiev emerged from the 1950s as an establishment composer of the USSR. Indeed, young musicians electrified by the new permissiveness of the Khrushchev Thaw often found Prokofiev's conservatism suffocating, as the musicologist Peter Schmelz has shown.[12]

Finally able to return to his life's work, Nestyev found that he needed to change little. His glowing review of the 1939 premiere of the *Nevsky* Cantata (noted in chapter 4) was reprinted unchanged in a 1955 book entitled *Soviet Symphonic Music*, as if the nadir of 1948 were a dream.[13] In a separate chapter in the same volume, Nestyev acknowledged many positives in Prokofiev's output during the last two decades of his life—his Soviet years, in other words—but the *Nevsky* Cantata was "the pride of Soviet music, one of its acknowledged summits." Yet he also tried to appropriate some of the film's cultural cachet, describing how Prokofiev's music had inspired a group of Black Sea sailors who watched the film during the defense of Sevastopol, sheltered from German bombs in an underground room. "Of Prokofiev's works, none attained the political relevance of *Alexander Nevsky*," Nestyev pointed out, veering back to the cantata to conclude that "it is difficult to overestimate the significance the *Alexander Nevsky* Cantata holds for all of Soviet music."[14] At least in its concert setting, Prokofiev's *Nevsky* was a classic rooted a historical moment perpetuated as state-unifying myth. It had attained a kind of relevance critics referred to as "contemporaneity" (*sovremennost*). Other Soviet writers followed Nestyev's lead. Marina Sabinina, for example, advanced Nestyev's conceit that *Nevsky* had reawakened Prokofiev's national voice, parroting even the details of her colleague's argument; both, for example, assert that fleeting glimpses of a mature national voice grace the Third Piano Concerto (1921).[15]

We might want to dismiss such writing as ideological puffery. Yet it did important work in the Soviet context. It positioned the *Nevsky* Cantata as Prokofiev's pivot from cosmopolitanism to nationalism, sectioning the composer's output into two groups, one ideologically suspect and the other classic; one bourgeois and Western, the other Russian. While outwardly celebrating *Nevsky*'s contemporaneousness and accessibility, moreover, it mobilized familiar high-art values. The cantata, spun as a venerable genre renewed by Prokofiev, got the attention instead of the film score. In this way, authors emphasized Prokofiev's individual agency. Nestyev fails even to mention Eisenstein's name in the chapter he wrote for the 1955 volume, let alone acknowledge the music's collaborative origins. Prokofiev's status as individual creative genius was thus secured, even if it was divested of the autonomy and innovation with which such a concept is often associated in the West.

THEORIZING, MYTHOLOGIZING

Eisenstein died of a heart attack on the morning of February 11, 1948. Prokofiev, still reeling from the shock of the Zhdanov resolution, declared "with the death of Sergei Mikhailovich Eisenstein, I consider my cinematic career forever finished."[16] At least that is what Boris Volsky recalled when he wrote his impressions of the Prokofiev-Eisenstein collaboration in 1954. Authors have rehearsed this soundbite ever since, as it efficiently conveys a depth of artistic partnership that has come to symbolize Eisenstein and Prokofiev's work together. Writers often treat the collaboration as a "phenomenon," to borrow Royal S. Brown's description, one that was innovative, experimental, and visionary—in short, values strikingly opposed to those of Socialist Realism.[17] The seeds of this particular narrative are, perhaps not surprisingly, found in the Stakhanovite claims we noted in chapter 2, particularly Tissé's and Eisenstein's technological innovations, Prokofiev's microphone experiments, and the dramatic pace of the production. Eisenstein's theorizing, much of it done after *Nevsky*'s production, further advanced the sense of innovation and experimentation. This narrative grew to be one essentially opposed to that of Nestyev and others who actively minimized Eisenstein's role in Prokofiev's achievement and focused on the cantata—the music "itself." Like the Socialist Realist narrative, however, the collaborative narrative served a variety of ends.

Eisenstein's theoretical imagination was a laboratory in which he continued to work on his films long after their premieres, envisaging new audiovisual possibilities and models for their analysis. His work with Prokofiev occasioned one of his most famous essays, "Vertical Montage," a post-production rumination on the possibilities of combining sound, music, and image. The heart of the essay is a storyboard-like assemblage of seventeen bars of Prokofiev's cue "Daybreak," shown in piano reduction beneath twelve horizontally positioned stills taken from the visual sequence the music accompanies (figure 5.1). Eisenstein proposed correspondences, or "counterpoint," as he described it, between the shapes traced by melodic lines in the musical notation and visual outlines in the stills. The analysis encodes musical gesture and movement (or lack of it). For example, Eisenstein insists that the rising quarter notes of shot 1 furnish forward motion—an intensification—whose emotional impact is similar to the axial cut, or sudden zoom in, between shots 1 and 2. The axial cut itself causes a comparable emotional intensification by drawing the viewer closer to the action. Similarly, the stasis of the insistent D sharps in the fourth measure of the music (the repeated eighth notes in the middle of the

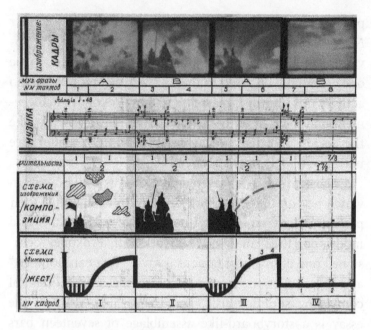

FIGURE 5.1 Diagram from Sergei Eisenstein's essay "Vertical Montage"
(first four frames only). From *top to bottom* the categories listed
at left are: depiction: shots, musical phrases / measure number,
music, duration, scheme of depiction (composition), scheme of
movement (gesture), shot number. Sergei M. Eisenstein, *The Film
Sense*, trans. and ed. Jay Leyda (New York: Harcourt, Brace, 1942).

staff) is the musical equivalent of the flatness of the horizon
in shot 4.[18]

Eisenstein's claims about the successful integration
of music and image in the film did not go uncontested.
Hanns Eisler and Theodor Adorno, positing that the scene
in question was an entirely mainstream pairing of evoc-
ative music and image, ridiculed the analysis as "heavy
artillery to shoot sparrows." [19] Claudia Gorbman branded
it a "delirium" that confuses shot composition and musical movement.[20] But Eisenstein asked difficult questions.

How can an artist synthesize image and music without one being slave to the other? How do musical gestures or images combine to create something greater, just as disparate visual images can be edited to create meaning not inherent in any of the constituent parts? Eisenstein wanted a way to theorize the visuality of Prokofiev's music, just as he spoke of edited images as a musical staff of visuals. His questions might concern ballet theorists interested in movement; they had also been asked by Richard Wagner, Alexander Scriabin, and others preoccupied with unifying the arts. Conceivably, Eisenstein anticipated a polemical debate. "We are looking for *commensurability*, and not illustration or reduplication," he bristled in an unpublished response to Eisler and Adorno.[21] He mocked Walt Disney's animation of Prokofiev's *Peter and the Wolf* (included in the 1946 collection *Make Mine Music*) because "a quacking duck, a cat, a bird, a wolf, Peter" in Prokofiev's score had only visual equivalents. He told his students that if they remained "in the realm of *structures*," they would fail to find "*an illustrative correspondence between the essences* of the musical movement and the movement of the image."[22]

Perhaps Eisenstein sensed his theorizing might be confused with his working method. In "Vertical Montage," he described the latter, insofar as it involved Prokofiev, as nothing more than intuition. Many of the results, he noted, "coincided so well with the 'inner resonance' linking music and pictures that they now seem to have been the most carefully 'prearranged' combinations." Unable to explain the nature of this intuition, Eisenstein poeticized it in a literary portrait titled "PRKFV" that he drafted in 1942 and completed in 1947.[23] In this oft-cited piece, Eisenstein insists that Prokofiev mobilized a complex, emotionally inflected mnemonic system to divine, with clock-like efficiency, the musical equivalent of a visual sequence. Some passages in Eisenstein's essay are purposely mystifying, and the more banal practicalities we observed in chapter 2 (e.g., scenario discussions, Prokofiev's "blocking" method) are nowhere in evidence. Rather, in a tone of wonder, Eisenstein comes to self-serving conclusions, insisting, for example, that "the repetition of groups of expressive combinations so necessary in music is no different than the ways in which image unfolds in rhythmic and montage groups."[24] There is a great deal of willful exaggeration as well, with Eisenstein and Prokofiev "squabbling" over whether music or image should come first. Like his theoretical writings, Eisenstein's literary portraits often envisage an ideal rather than document reality.

Prokofiev also indulged in some spin, as we have already seen. In the 1939 essay noted in chapter 2, he portrayed his work on Nevsky's recording as a technological breakthrough. For instance, he described making the Teutonic trumpets sound "ice-coated" by lowering microphones in front of the brass section, the resulting distortion yielding "an extraordinarily dramatic effect." This and similar examples constituted an "inverted orchestration" that allowed for combinations "unthinkable in music for concert performance."[25] These were hardly discoveries. Prokofiev had employed them with little fanfare at least five years earlier in his work on *Lieutenant Kijé*, and in the meantime far more sophisticated technology had dazzled him in Hollywood.

While not denying their theoretical and documentary merits, we can see how Eisenstein's and Prokofiev's writings have functioned as subtle propaganda. Tatiana Egorova, the author of the only English-language survey of Soviet film music, asserts that *Alexander Nevsky* "broke down all established stereotypes and notions of the ways in which music and representation should interact, and it was built as a complex polyphonic composition."[26] The collaboration also paved the way for "visual music," she claims, referencing an experimental field that uses music to structure visual image. Although she includes Eisenstein's analysis as a figure in her book, she avoids engaging with it as she describes the ways in which Prokofiev's music supports the film's overall plot. Concluding, she refers opaquely to the development of "forms of music and representation synthesis on the basis of their image synchronization, or counterpoint" as if this accomplishment needed no explanation.[27] Such an approach seems to do little other than assert the value, vis-à-vis innovation and experimentation, of a film whose wide appeal derived from its studied simplicity. Egorova is hardly alone. It is common to identify *Nevsky* as "a breakthrough in audio-visual montage" without any further explanation, as John Riley does in his study of Shostakovich's film music.[28] In his classic study *Overtones and Undertones*, Royal S. Brown engages Eisenstein's analysis in more rigorous fashion, convincingly demonstrating how Eisenstein's editing in *Ivan the Terrible*—for which Prokofiev also wrote a musical score—forged non-narrative audiovisual connections of the type theorized in "Vertical Montage." Yet he believes an unsubstantiated assertion by one of Eisenstein's biographers that, while working on

Alexander Nevsky, Prokofiev had in some cases rewritten a passage as many as six times to achieve Eisenstein's goals. On that basis, Brown implies that the kind of sophisticated theorizing in "Vertical Montage" was behind the execution of *Alexander Nevsky*, rather than the rapid-fire, occasionally messy progression we observed in chapter 2.[29] Significantly, *Nevsky* enters Brown's historical narrative of film music not as an example of effective state propaganda but as a brilliant demonstration of structuring according to musical principles. This perspective now pervades the popular imagination; during an intermission spot of a televised BBC Proms performance of *Nevsky* in 2011, for instance, critic and Prokofiev biographer David Nice highlighted Eisenstein's sophisticated analysis, in essence asserting its relevance to the audience's listening experience despite the fact that it was the cantata, and not the film score, that was performed on the program.[30]

Prokofiev's thoughts on "inverted orchestration," although hardly the theoretical tour-de-force of Eisenstein's "Vertical Montage," have left a similar trace in both Soviet and Western literature. Sergei Morozov, for example, the author of a 1967 biography of Prokofiev in the popular series of Soviet publications Lives of Remarkable People, bizarrely introduces a discussion of the *Nevsky* Cantata with a lengthy description of the microphone techniques Prokofiev employed only in Mosfilm's recording hall.[31] He seems to include this framing for the same reason Egorova dressed up her discussion with an image of Eisenstein's analysis. And what of Nestyev, our hero in the Soviet realm? In his 1972 biography of Prokofiev (his fourth and final), he is so eager to prove the cantata's innovations that he refers

to the entirely pedestrian string mute as an agent of "defor-
mation" and credits Prokofiev's equally common directive
in distanza (in the distance) to the technical innovations
of sound recording.[32] Elsewhere he describes the cantata's
"bold contrapuntal dual-plane methods, which by striking cinematographic effects are transferred to the realm of
symphonic music."[33] Here he referred to the alternation of
German and Russian themes in the Battle on Ice, which,
at least in his original 1939 review, he had insisted was an
extension of nineteenth-century models. More recently,
the musicologist Rebecca Schwartz-Bishir has argued that
Prokofiev's battery of studio recording techniques constituted a modernist angle by which Prokofiev achieved a self-
satisfying rapprochement with or possibly even subversion
of the rules of Socialist Realism.[34]

Eisenstein asked probing questions, but in the process he
also transformed *Nevsky*'s agitprop into an apolitical, theoretical ideal. In his theoretical work, sight and sound are
treated as abstractions stripped of their social and political
context. But lingering on Prokofiev's technological innovations or Eisenstein's audiovisual sophistication does similar
work, distancing the film from qualities associated with
Socialist Realism, middlebrow art, and propaganda. In
other words, it rescues *Alexander Nevsky* from the trash bin
to which so much Soviet propaganda has been consigned.

AN "INDEPENDENT LIFE" IN THE WEST

In 1943, the English musicologist Gerald Abraham, a vet-
eran watcher of Russian music, included Prokofiev in
his *Eight Soviet Composers*, a slim volume offered as an

up-to-date overview of Soviet composition. For nearly ten of the book's 102 pages, he lingers on the *Nevsky* Cantata, a work he clearly admired for its evocations of nineteenth-century national classics such as Rimsky-Korsakov's *Sadko* and Borodin's *Prince Igor*. He complained only of the fifth movement (the Battle on Ice), which he found too illustrative and insufficiently reworked for the concert stage, reminding him that "film-music in the concert hall is the worst kind of programme-music."[35] In the course of a largely unremarkable analysis, however, he answered those who wondered if Prokofiev's accessible, high-Romantic style had been forced. "The truth is," he asserted, "that [Prokofiev] had already been tending in this direction for some time.... Prokofiev's development has not suffered very severely by his decision to return to his native land." Simplicity and lyricism had eclipsed "his old pungency," Abraham admitted, but Prokofiev now seemed to be nourishing an "epic vein" he had long neglected. Apropos the gains and losses of repatriation to Russia, Abraham found it "difficult to decide which are the more considerable."[36] Writing in England at the height of the Second World War, Abraham easily skirted the question of *Nevsky*'s origins in the propaganda machine of his country's ally. More striking, however, is his ambivalence on Soviet creative "restrictions," which hardly seemed a negative if they had renewed Prokofiev's art.

If time and place colored Abraham's comments, so too did they shape Andrey Olkhovsky's impressions of Prokofiev's work. An émigré musicologist working in the United States, Olkhovsky turned out his own comprehensive study of Soviet music in 1955 at the behest of the

Research Program on the USSR, one of the many know-your-enemy projects that sprang up during the Cold War (this one based at Columbia University). Leaving little to the reader's imagination, he titled his book *Music under the Soviets: The Agony of an Art*. His account was partisan, tendentious, and therefore eminently influential in the polarized political climate. Here is Olkhovsky on the political corruption of large choral forms in Soviet music:

> The extensive cultivation of small musical forms, particularly the mass-song, with the obvious aim of reducing music to a means of political propaganda, has had a noticeable effect on large choral forms such as the oratorio and the cantata. In the actual practice of Soviet composers, however, these "larger forms" are in reality nothing but augmented mass-songs.[37]

But, on the very next page:

> The magnificent description of the "Battle on the Ice," the final chorus, "Arise Ye Russian People" ... and the deeply mournful episode of the "Field of the Dead," written in the style of ancient lamentation—passages such as these make [the *Nevsky* Cantata] unquestionably the best ever written by a Soviet composer in this form. Naturally, therefore, this work is no way corresponds to the standard propagandistic definition of the cantata.[38]

Naturally for whom? If Prokofiev's creation is "unquestionably the best," then is it ipso facto unsullied by politics? It was simple for Olkhovsky to dismiss Prokofiev's *Cantata for the Twentieth Anniversary of October* and *Zdravitsa*, works whose texts extolled communism and Stalin, respectively.

"Insincere, forced, and antimusical," he cautioned readers who had never heard and likely never would hear them. But major American orchestras had already added the *Nevsky* Cantata to their repertoires, and Olkhovsky could switch on the radio and occasionally catch a broadcast of the work. Thus he turned for help to the hoariest of the nineteenth-century Romanticist tropes, the conviction that great art is by definition transcendent. We already sensed something of this ingrained belief in the previous chapter, festering as it does behind the anxiety over patriotism in the concert hall. Recall that ten years earlier Olin Downes had recommended the cantata because it was unadorned, visceral, here-and-now stuff. A decade later, Olkhovsky insisted that readers should value the work precisely because it lacked those qualities. Yet both critics shared the goal of extending permission to their readers to enjoy the work; whether American audiences felt they needed such license is a different question.

As the Cold War escalated, other writers came to share Olkhovsky's convictions. In his influential 1960 biography, for example, French critic Claude Samuel insisted that the *Nevsky* Cantata "was able to liberate itself magnificently from the context of the picture," yielding "one of the most imposing and dramatic of Soviet works." [39] Samuel's example inspired later authors such as Lawrence Hanson, who maintained that *Nevsky* "was given an independent life by the cantata" and was thus rescued from the "crudity and falsity" of Eisenstein's film. [40] (Predictably, Samuel and his imitators dismiss Prokofiev's comparatively obscure occasional works and political oratorios, soft-pedaling their stylistic resemblance to *Nevsky*.) Likewise, Jay S. Harrison, music critic for the *New York Herald Tribune*, asserted that Prokofiev "went pretty much his own way." "Far from being merely an adjunct to a motion picture," he reasoned,

> each episode [of the cantata] has a granite-like musical strength carved out of the firmest musical logic. Bold, grand, vigorous and moving is every measure of the *Alexander Nevsky* cantata, and because of this I am willing to take an oath that once you have gained acquaintance with it you will never again approach film music in quite the same way.[41]

These comments, made in the liner notes for Fritz Reiner's celebrated 1960 recording with the Chicago Symphony for RCA Victor's high fidelity "Shaded Dog" series, were inserted in a jacket whose cover art itself suggested degrees of abstraction from the film. Federico Castellón's painting on the cover conveys something of Eisenstein's film (figure 5.2), but the angular, modernist, and black-and-white image on the jacket's reverse (figure 5.3, identified only as "Heroes" by "Ross") suggests a far more abstract, unspecific frame for listening to the cantata. All of these examples insist that the narrative of Eisenstein's film, like the words of Prokofiev's other, "insincere" and "anti-musical" cantatas, was the dead weight that hindered the music's ascent to the apolitical clouds of high art. So much better, then, that Prokofiev himself cast it off in 1939 when he transferred the *Nevsky* music from screen to stage.

By 1968, the soil had been prepared for some hot-house myth growing. That year Victor Seroff's *Sergei Prokofiev: A Soviet Tragedy* appeared, a hefty accounting of Prokofiev's career that would hold sway in the Anglophone world for the next twenty years. After a lengthy and anodyne

FIGURE 5.2   Jacket cover (front) of RCA Victor Red Seal LM-2395 (1960).

narration of both Eisenstein's and Prokofiev's comments on *Alexander Nevsky*, Seroff breezily asserted that the film's "long-lasting success is no doubt partly due to its being one of the most musical films ever produced. In 1941, when Hitler's armies invaded Russia, the film—*a purely artistic achievement*—gained additional significance: political, and as a timely patriotic manifestation of the Russian people." [42] Here is willful amnesia, the film's origins glossed over and its propagandistic import, now separated from its "artistic achievement," restyled as a coincidence of war. Seroff seems to say that with the film's political moment now more than

Prokofieff *ALEXANDER NEVSKY* Reiner/Chicago Symphony/Rosalind Elias, Mezzo-soprano

FIGURE 5.3   Jacket cover (reverse) of RCA Victor Red Seal LM-2395 (1960).

two decades in the past, we can forget about Soviet wartime patriotism and other transient things. The *Nevsky*
Cantata is mentioned by Seroff only as a pivot to discussion
of Prokofiev's "most humiliating work," his 1939 birthday
gift to Stalin, *Zdravitsa*. Seroff derided the source of much
of his own information—Israel Nestyev—for identifying
in this cantata the same "Russian character" that pervades
Nevsky. Yet for Seroff, the mere fact that *Zdravitsa*'s text glorified Stalin excused him from engaging with the cantata's
music (in which there are indeed many similarities to the
Nevsky Cantata).[43] The same sentiment found its way into

specialist studies by way of Stanley D. Krebs, who branded *Zdravitsa* an ideological and musical failure in his book on the development of Soviet music.[44]

In a way, all of these examples concern not Prokofiev himself but rather opposing critical constructions of Prokofiev. For Soviet critics there was the pre- and post-repatriation Prokofiev, the former misguided, the latter a classic. For Western critics, there was the true Prokofiev, one rhetorically extracted and thus spared from his Soviet context (he was a modernist, apolitical, purely artistic, and a craftsman par excellence), and there was the other Prokofiev, one who tossed off occasional political hack-work. Reviewing Harlow Robinson's 1987 biography of Prokofiev for the *New York Review of Books*, for example, the composer Arthur Berger asserted his own view that

> Prokofiev could write the music he wanted to write as long as he fulfilled his political responsibility by turning out accepta-ble occasional pieces—his "public" efforts, most of them choral, with texts glorifying the official cause. He does not seem to have thought much of these works. His "private" works employed the skills he had mastered at home before the Revolution and ben-efited from the experience he had acquired abroad.

How does Berger know so well what Prokofiev thought? Or is the thought that Prokofiev willing to (or *wanted* to!) write these works simply incompatible with a worldview that cherishes transcendent, unfettered art?[45]

The notion of the bifurcated composer from Eastern Europe was a Cold War staple. Soviet critics embraced Igor Stravinsky's early ballets such as *The Firebird* (1910) and *Petrushka* (1911), steeped as they were in Russian folklore, but drew the line at the composer's nationally unmarked neoclassical works of the 1920s, all written after his emigration from Russia. In an insightful study, Danielle Fosler-Lussier has shown that following his death in 1945, Western critics and Eastern Bloc ideologues neatly divided up Béla Bartók's output, the former group claiming Bartók was himself only in his most complex modernist efforts while the latter said the same of his more accessible and folklore-based efforts.[46] These examples belie, however, the occasional distance between critical and performance canons. Among the most popular of Bartók's works in the West was the *Concerto for Orchestra* (1943), the jewel in the crown of the "folklore" camp and a work often derided by Western critics as evidence of a populist renunciation of modernism.

But the concert hall, with its high-art foundations, uprooted music from its original contexts and functions just as powerfully as any critic could. Consider the wonder of Peter J. Rabinowitz, a writer who annotated a 1981 American release of Evgeny Svetlanov's recording of the *Nevsky* Cantata on the Melodiya label. "The popularity of *Alexander Nevsky* has been so great," he remarked,

> that even in times of strained relations between the United States and the Soviet Union, American performers have taken up this model of Soviet patriotism with enthusiasm. I have even heard it performed in Chicago's Grant Park, where the neon signs of American oil companies blinked down over a chorus shouting out, in English, 'Arise, ye Russian People!' Prokofiev, a composer who almost never lost his sense of humor, would have appreciated that irony.[47]

CHAPTER 6

NEVSKY
AFTER THE USSR

I N HIS 1991 SATIRICAL fantasy *On Mozart*, Anthony Burgess imagines a meeting of Beethoven, Wagner, Prokofiev, and other departed composers in heaven. Prokofiev, who still observes earthly time, suspects the gathering is to celebrate the one hundredth anniversary of his birth. Instead, Beethoven runs on about the "Mozartian ideal of purity," Wagner spews nationalist epithets, and all gripe that it was Mozart whom god chose to sit at his right hand. "I understood I was to be celebrated," Prokofiev indignantly protests. Arthur Bliss, an English composer of modest earthly fame, hisses in reply, "You already are, and perhaps more than you ought to be. You abased yourself before the bloodthirsty Stalin. You placed the philistine state before the call of your individual talent." "I resent that," Prokofiev replies, without contesting the accusation.[1] Good art is above politics, Bliss insinuates, his bile betraying jealousy at the popular success Prokofiev enjoyed (purchased at a terrible cost, he would hasten to add). Burgess knew that good satire is only a modest exaggeration of reality, and here that reality concerns the values we encountered in the last chapter: Romantic values nourished by the ideological divisions of the Cold War.

The centenary of Prokofiev's birth in 1991 was largely ignored on earth as it was in Burgess's heaven, yet under far less humorous circumstances. As Burgess's book went to press, the Soviet Union ceased to exist, fracturing into its constituent republics following Mikhail Gorbachev's resignation on December 25. The Soviet became the post-Soviet; pundits in the West declared "victory" in the Cold War; and the Iron Curtain, that metaphor of ideological and intellectual divisions, seemed at last to part. We might expect that as contexts rapidly shifted, the place of *Alexander Nevsky* within them would too, particularly in the former Soviet Union, where both film and cantata had been so closely aligned with Soviet officialdom. In some cases, this change was very real. In others, *Nevsky*'s place remained stubbornly constant. For unlike Soviet Communism, Romantic values would emerge from the Cold War unscathed.

NEVSKY *RECONSIDERED*

Five years after the Soviet Union crumbled, the German biographer Maria Biesold turned her attention to Prokofiev. Summarizing the accolades the *Nevsky* film and cantata had enjoyed on both sides of the Iron Curtain, she sounded a jarring note of caution:

> But the great victory and the many enthusiastic reviews of the film, a successful film work of art, cannot hide, even at today's remove, that Prokofiev wrote music for a garish, chauvinistic work of propaganda. The music's creative power and simplistic portrayals of the characters serve a drama that appears more than questionable.[2]

Sounding like an academic version of Burgess's Arthur Bliss, Biesold challenges Prokofiev's *Nevsky* on ethical grounds, a position largely absent from more than a half century of writing on the music. Not surprisingly, *Alexander Nevsky* had a contentious history in Biesold's native country. In West Germany, the film first played only in 1963, having been heavily edited to remove portrayals of German cruelty. Although the premiere of the complete film followed three years later, *Nevsky*'s anti-German content clearly remained potent.[3] Whether that potency derived from outright offense or the common postwar sense that the National Socialist years were an aberration best forgotten is difficult to discern. Nevertheless, Biesold seems to challenge those who find satisfaction in a "more than questionable" drama.

The English composer William Walton might have felt pity for Prokofiev had he lived long enough to read Biesold's biography. He made it no secret that *Nevsky* had danced in his imagination when he prepared to compose the score for *Henry V* (1944), Laurence Olivier's screen version of Shakespeare's play. The film's heart is a fifteen-minute battle sequence depicting the English victory at Agincourt, one for which Walton, following Prokofiev, composed music in advance that is indebted to his Soviet colleague's form and style. Unlike *Nevsky, Henry V* was not a state commission, nor was Olivier expected to support an orthodox ideology. Nevertheless, England's Ministry of Information recognized the wartime propaganda value of the stirring historical tale of English struggle and victory at Agincourt (even if it was a long-passed victory, like Nevsky's), and during production it released Olivier and a handful of the film's actors from active duty. Indeed, Walton's accessibility and *narodnost* would have pleased the most conservative Soviet bureaucrat; the film score's style evokes more of the "national" Edward Elgar rather than anything of the film's fifteenth-century setting, just as Prokofiev called to mind Rimsky-Korsakov rather than thirteenth-century liturgical music. Walton, again like his Soviet colleague, also highlighted the "unusually complex and close collaboration of sound and screen from one bar, or visual movement, to the next." And, riding a wave of popular acclaim, he extracted a suite from the film that the BBC Proms featured already in 1945, a year after the film's premiere. As the Cold War unfolded, Walton's music sounded regularly, both on screen and stage.[4]

Despite the striking similarities, Walton has never been called to task for debasing his art. Perhaps the reason lies in the crucial differences between the two films: the source of *Henry V*'s script was Shakespeare, not a Communist Party darling of dubious renown. Or perhaps Prokofiev, more widely known internationally, is held to higher standards as a greater genius, his transgression of the art/politics firewall considered more criminal than Walton's. Discussions of comparisons like these invariably narrow in on the problematic divide between the creation and reception of music. We might contemplate, for example, to what extent a work's original context can or should determine a listener's experience of the work in a different context. The German composer Carl Orff's cantata *Carmina Burana* (1936) was a favorite among Nazi officials, even though its text did not extoll Nazi ideology (just as that of the *Nevsky* Cantata was not specific to communism or Stalinism). In contemporary popular culture, *Carmina Burana*'s opening chorus "O Fortuna" appears in a range of contexts, from episodes of *The Simpsons* and *The Rachel Maddow Show* to New England Patriots games.[5] In all of these contexts, the chorus's rousing, unrelentingly rhythmic character stokes the enthusiasm of crowds of football fans, just as it galvanized groups of Nazi supporters. Propaganda does not modify ideas but rather provokes action, as the French philosopher Jacques Ellul insisted in his classic study of attitude formation.[6] Walton and Prokofiev both lent their talent to the same action, namely, fostering the kind of group affiliation needed to support xenophobic patriotism or wartime readiness. Insofar as patriotism reflects back onto the state, Walton ennobled Churchill's England and Prokofiev glorified Stalin's Russia, a glaring difference for observers in different contexts and with different political allegiances.

Biesold was not alone in challenging the popularity of Prokofiev's *Nevsky* music. Following a 1991 performance of the cantata by Kurt Masur and the San Francisco Symphony, the musicologist Richard Taruskin wondered about such a "crude display of Stalinist triumphalism" coming on the heels of the fall of the Berlin Wall and the teetering of Eastern Bloc communist regimes. The ovation that followed suggested that "no political message at all had been received, just a rousing piece of music," he complained in the *New York Times*.[7] His concern was formalism, the focus on a work's internal coherence and craft at the expense of its function. By 1991, the *Nevsky* Cantata in the West had long been detached from its Soviet context, and the formalist critical maneuvering that brought it there had been far from passive, as we observed in the last chapter. Taruskin encouraged audiences to admit politics into their consideration of Prokofiev's art so they might see that the composer had, in fact, "played toady to the tyrant." Such clarity would portend a swift demise to Prokofiev's popularity in the West, he predicted.[8] Yet no such demise occurred. On the contrary, during the period that Taruskin and Biesold wrote, *Alexander Nevsky* emerged in yet another reformulated guise, one that further obfuscated the work's origins and opened the door to new functions, formalisms, and ideologies.

PROKOFIEV'S FILM ALEXANDER NEVSKY

The New York television producer John Goberman, known from shows such as *Live from Lincoln Center*, had long been an admirer of the *Nevsky* Cantata. The film in which it originated was another story; the worn copies available in the United States provided little for eyes or ears. Through considerable persistence in the mid-1980s, the early years of Gorbachev's reforms, Goberman secured a new print of the original nitrate negative from the State Film Archive outside Moscow. Armed with restored images, he convinced the composer and arranger William Brohn to reconstruct the film's score. Unlike the cantata, the *Nevsky* film score had never been published, and the handful of pages of manuscript that survived the war were interred in a closed Moscow archive. Thus, through persistence equal to Goberman's, Brohn reconstructed the score by ear, his only help a copy of the *Nevsky* Cantata score from which he worked backward through the process Prokofiev had carried forward in January 1939. Goberman and Brohn's ultimate goal was even more ambitious, however: a showing of the new print accompanied by live orchestra. Andre Previn, having just recorded the *Nevsky* Cantata with the Los Angeles Philharmonic, took up the challenge of such a "film-concert" during the Philharmonic's 1987–88 season. On November 3, Los Angeles audiences saw Eisenstein's images projected on a massive screen in the Dorothy Chandler Pavilion while the Philharmonic played in perfect synchronization on a semi-darkened stage beneath. An ovation followed, just as it did later in the same season in Cleveland (the Cleveland Orchestra with Vladimir Ashkenazy) and Washington (the National Symphony Orchestra with Mstislav Rostropovich).[9]

The press billed these performances as "Prokofiev's *Alexander Nevsky.*" Though the film had been returned to the sounds of Prokofiev's soundtrack, it remained ancillary to music performed by musicians executing a feat of coordination front and center on the stage. Prokofiev's music had feebly croaked from cinema speakers for fifty years; now it roared forth from a live orchestra more than three times the size of the ad hoc group employed for the original soundtrack. As Goberman explained, he and Brohn also allowed themselves some artistic license. They included an overture that featured "Arise, Ye Russian People," which, as Goberman explained, was "to focus the audience's attention on the conductor, orchestra and chorus." And even though Prokofiev's microphone effects had attracted so much attention over the years, they had little place in a concert work, where "an undistorted sound would be more effective." Goberman also asked Brohn to replace "the unfortunate trombone glissando which had accompanied the final slide of the last German under the ice with a somewhat more dignified descending brass."[10] Justifying these modifications, Goberman suggested that he and Brohn were tracking closer to what Prokofiev "intended," given that *Nevsky*'s original soundtrack had so poorly conveyed the composer's music.[11] Many conductors, such as Michael Lankester (who led performances of the Goberman-Brohn reconstruction with the National Symphony during 1989–90), echoed this rationale. "What we are attempting to do for the first time in history," he told audiences, "is to do what Prokofiev intended."[12] Invoking Prokofiev's authority was a great selling point, but it also perpetuated the music's autonomy as a musical *work*. Eisenstein's images may have had something to say about Germans and Russians, but the focus fell on Prokofiev's craft. As such, the newest *Nevsky* work proved as malleable in differing contexts as the cantata had during the Second World War.

During the rapid changes that followed the fall of the Berlin Wall, commentators often lingered on universal themes that could be pinned to the undeniable emotional impact of the new *Nevsky* film-concert. And they had plenty of opportunity to do so; by the early 1990s Previn's initial performance had been duplicated more than fifty times across the United States and Western Europe. Reviewing a much-trumpeted performance at Lincoln Center in New York, Edward Rothstein argued that what he saw

> was more a nationalist film—Eisenstein called it a "patriotic weapon"—than a Stalinist one. Prokofiev's music is also far from institutional or bombastic. When Janis Taylor sang the lyrical lament after the ice battle on Friday night, the chill was one of human sympathy, not political correctness, despite the labored text.[13]

The same moment of human sympathy moved the *Washington Post* critic Joseph McLellan to write that

> a movie does not constantly have to be subtle, complex or technically dazzling to be a masterpiece. What it does have to do is embody a vision and communicate compellingly with its audience. "Nevsky" does that. It not only spoke to its primary audience, the Russian people, in the 1930s—it speaks still to a universal audience. It not only delivered Joseph Stalin's original messages: that those who invade Russia will die and that it is glorious to defend your homeland. It conveys more universal messages about the horror and pity—and, yes, exhilaration—of war; the strength, ingenuity and resiliency of little people in the grip of monstrous forces; the simple joy and anguish of being human together.[14]

Following a repeat performance a year later, the same critic perhaps overstated his case, writing that Stalin never came to mind. "Instead," he insisted, "I couldn't help thinking of a hotter climate and the sands of Kuwait."[15] Here was a victory of universality that might have impressed even Prokofiev, the themes of his music so generalized that they seemed to speak to the Gulf War that was just two days old when McClellan recorded his thoughts. But what do these comments capture if not a newfound sense of what a Soviet critic might have praised as "contemporaneity"?

Goberman's project also reanimated the Cold War rhetoric of technological sophistication that we traced in previous chapters. The project was an immense undertaking; even with the Los Angeles Philharmonic players coaxed into donating their time (the initial performance was billed as a fundraiser), the price tag for the first three performances in 1987–88 exceeded three hundred thousand dollars.[16] Accounts of the early performances consistently boasted of the complex stage setup, particularly a four-track magnetic soundtrack that delivered dialogue, sound effects, and English-language subtitles (projected on a second screen), and—most importantly—coordinated with a computer-controlled clock that fed cues to the conductor. Perhaps the prominent role of technology convinced officials at the American telecommunications company AT&T to underwrite the project. Whatever their motivations, they saddled Prokofiev's music with an entirely new message. As an executive with the company crowed, "We are pleased with the opportunity to offer 'Alexander Nevsky' as an important instrument of communication, understanding, diplomacy and peace reaffirming President Reagan's commitment to international cultural and educational projects."[17] This was quite a lofty aim for sound and image that originated as Stalinist propaganda.

AT&T based their sponsorship on the expectation that Previn's performance and those that followed would draw huge audiences. The company's executives were presumably pleased. Reflecting on the moment, a senior vice president at IMG Artists, a London-based management company, called the *Nevsky* film-concert premiere a "light-bulb" moment, one that suggested an antidote to the plague of dwindling concert audiences. Soon other film-concerts followed, and today one can regularly find anything from MGM classics to Hitchcock to Tim Burton's *The Nightmare before Christmas* on the stages of major symphony orchestras. Goberman himself went on to produce *The Wizard of Oz, Casablanca, Singin' in the Rain,* and *Psycho,* to list just a few of his many titles. "The very best of this music can be accepted on its own, purely musical, terms," reasoned the British conductor John Wilson. Appeals to highbrow values such as Wilson's justified the presence of such music in concert halls to audiences, but the financial managers of major orchestras needed no such assistance. A half century after its premiere in Stalin's Russia, Eisenstein and Prokofiev's work had launched a movement that has since revitalized the concert seasons of major orchestras in the United States and Europe.[18]

NEVSKY *RETURNS HOME*

Alexander Nevsky in its various forms has remained popular in post-Soviet Russia. Seeking to explain its continued viability in a radically different context, the Russian historian Yuri Krivosheev suggested that as propaganda *Nevsky* mobilized patriotism rather than anything as specific as state socialism.[19] Perhaps, but the stabilizing reference point of Russian history in moments of national identity crisis should not be underestimated. For instance, in 1991, as the Soviet Union crumbled, Georgii Kuznetsov produced *The Life of Alexander Nevsky*, a historical drama that chronicled Alexander's final days. And in 2008, at the conclusion of Vladimir Putin's first presidency, Igor Kalenov made *Alexander: The Neva Battle*, a ten-million-dollar blockbuster that dramatized Alexander's 1240 victory at the River Neva. When asked why he chose to produce a film that undoubtedly would be compared to Eisenstein's *Alexander Nevsky*, Kalenov cited the many difficult decisions Alexander had to make. "I am certain that our society today is in need of historical examples that demonstrate compromises are necessary to address global challenges," he told a reporter. "Alexander was strong, smart, cunning," he added, insisting that the last quality was a positive one and "extremely useful for a politician."[20] That a "strong cult of personality" had been renewed in Putin's Russia did not pass by critic Larisa Maliukova, who derided the film as "our remake of 1938 ... without Prokofiev's grandeur and Eisenstein's talent." Government oversight of film was hardly like that of the Stalin era, she added, but that did not stop certain "rulers of cinema-dom" from currying favor with Russia's leadership.[21]

Eisenstein's and Prokofiev's *Alexander Nevsky* also came to reflect cultural concerns of the post-Soviet era. On November 29, 2004, a gala *Nevsky* film-concert drew Moscow's cultural elite to the Bolshoi Theater. They witnessed a new reconstruction by the German conductor Frank Strobel, who, benefiting from post-Soviet openness, had gained access to Prokofiev's fragmentary manuscripts. Although the result was not substantially different than Brohn's, the Moscow event was freighted with layers of significance. Foremost among these was the venue, the Bolshoi having been witness to the vagaries of the Stalin era. The first showing of the new anti-German film *Alexander Nevsky* in 1938 (albeit private), had taken place there. Only two years later, in display of pro-German sentiment catalyzed by the short-lived German-Soviet nonaggression pact, Eisenstein directed a production of Richard Wagner's *Die Walküre* at the Bolshoi. And on the very same stage in 2004, Strobel's *Alexander Nevsky* film-concert now crowned—absurdly for anyone who knew the film's history—a year-long celebration of German-Russian cultural friendship sponsored by the Foreign Office of the Federal Republic of Germany, the Russian Ministry of Culture, and other institutions.[22]

Many hopes had been pinned on the performance. Strobel had already been taken to task by German critics who complained that the 2003 German premiere had lacked proper historical contextualization and was in poor taste.[23] He was heartened by this criticism, he explained at a roundtable discussion following the Russian premiere, because his work had prompted discussion. "We must not forget our own history," he insisted.[24] Naum Kleiman, one of Russia's leading film experts, felt that the ovation at the end of the performance "was a sign that we are in a different historical phase, in a different historical stage." He hoped that the solemnity of the performance might return some "social significance" to the cinema that had been lost in recent decades.[25] The director of Moscow's Goethe Institute, a sponsor of the event, implied that the diplomatic efforts had generalized the film-concert's display of patriotism, claiming that "this film inspires us Germans to be patriots against the enemy."[26] The round-table discussion, which involved a handful of other cultural figures, was striking for its plurality of views. Placed into an ill-fitting and bizarre diplomatic frame, Eisenstein's images and Prokofiev's music seemed to have been detached from any stable reference point, becoming a malleable entity that could be wielded for any number of twenty-first-century concerns.

The Russian press documents an even more wide-ranging set of reactions. Some were predictable, such as Ekaterina Chen's argument that the performance showed an authentic Prokofiev, one not limited by 1938 recording technology.[27] By contrast, the critic Ekaterina Biriukova felt that an anti-German film, reconstructed and led by a German in Moscow's Bolshoi Theater, seemed at first blush to be "real masochism that, in the European world, truth be told, passes for self-scrutiny." Yet she implied that the transformative nature of the performance should not be underestimated. "The intrusion of live, modern sound into an old film ... turns it into a completely new, open structure unrelated to its original form, one open to new meanings."[28] Biriukova further noted that Strobel's reconstruction netted him the Order of *Saint* Alexander Nevsky, a sacred reformulation of the old Soviet official honor. In terms of new meanings and narratives, this award struck her as particularly significant, as it saddled a Soviet celluloid hero with a religious identity that Eisenstein had carefully avoided (the director worked in a country where atheism reigned, after all). For those more familiar with the cantata than the film, the gala performance of 2004 was a moment of discovery. For the critic Varvara Turova, learning that Prokofiev's familiar music fit specific visual sequences was a revelation, as she assumed it expressed only general themes of "mother Russia and loyalty to the motherland."[29] And, on the far end of the spectrum from Strobel and Kleiman's lofty hopes, many found the film too stagy and outdated. According to Turova, stifled laughter filled the hall when the audience beheld German knights tossing Russian children into a bonfire during the sack of Pskov.[30] The critic Svetlana Samoilova documented the same reaction, adding that the audience also seemed embarrassed by the flagrant patriotism of "Arise, Ye Russian People."[31]

Perhaps the most striking aspect of these heterogeneous creative convictions and critical reactions is what remained unacknowledged or unsaid: Stalin, communism, Socialist Realism, and the myriad other contextual factors that gave birth to *Alexander Nevsky* and shaped its meaning for the film's first audiences in 1938. At the same time, the late-twentieth-century search for Prokofiev's original "intent" through reconstruction seemed to fix Prokofiev and Eisenstein's work as a static artifact. So, too, did the Criterion Collection's lavish 2001 release of a restored *Alexander Nevsky* on DVD, as did the publication of Strobel's reconstruction by Sikorski Music Publishers in 2003, its pages making tangible the film score that had remained ephemeral for half of the twentieth century.

Yet Prokofiev's *Nevsky* has never been a static entity. It has been reconfigured as film score, cantata, and film-concert, not to mention myriad arrangements and extracts. Shuttled around the globe and presented in wildly different contexts, it has proved one of the last century's most malleable collections of sounds. Accordingly, *Alexander Nevsky* remains a stubbornly open space for cultivating diverse forms of collective identity. Initially, the music nurtured group identity within the Soviet Union. During the Second World War, its significance became transnational, a sonic marker of struggle and victory to be shared among the Allies. At the same time, the music, as interpreted and championed by Soviet critics, dictated an identity for Soviet music, one whose towering example demanded imitation. Not surprisingly, pretexts for performance and frames for reception have only grown more complex the farther we have traveled from our point of origin in 1938. As nearly three decades of film-concerts have demonstrated, contexts can be inadvertently or willfully banished, and new, trans-European, Orthodox, or capitalist frames called forth in their stead. If anything is static or fixed, it is the enduring appeal of Prokofiev's music. Eisenstein sensed this already in 1938 when he admired and wondered at the rhythmic drive and shape of Prokofiev's music, anticipating its role in a film that would, more than anything, galvanize its audiences. And so it has.

SERGEI PROKOFIEV, "MY CANTATA ALEXANDER NEVSKY"

P ROKOFIEV WROTE THE FOLLOWING *program note in March 1942 to accompany performances of the Alexander Nevsky Cantata in the United States. The English translation presumably made in 1942 does not survive; the following version is translated from the original Russian.*[1]

Alexander Nevsky's name is especially close to us now, in the days of patriotic war with German fascism. Seven hundred years ago, under the leadership of Alexander Nevsky, the Russian people defeated the German knights who invaded Russia. The 13th century was difficult for the Russian lands. Mongol hordes came from the east, seizing most of Russia's territory. And then from the west came hordes of German knights clad from head to toe in iron. They brought destruction and death. The Russian Prince Alexander was already famous for his victory over the Swedes in 1240 at the river Neva, for which he was called Nevsky. The choice therefore fell upon him as commander. The decisive battle with the Germans took place on April 5, 1242, on the ice of a great frozen lake near the city of

Pskov. Interestingly, the German forces back then formed a wedge, the tip of which plowed into their opponent, dividing it into two parts and destroying the separated flanks. Alexander Nevsky was familiar with this maneuver and positioned the weakest part of his forces in the center and moved the strongest forces to the sides. After the knights penetrated the center of the Russian forces, Alexander attacked them with the powerful force of his army's flanks. This maneuver caused confusion among the German ranks and sent them into a hasty retreat that ended in one of the most fascinating catastrophes of military history: when the heavy, iron-clad knights crowded near the bluff, the ice, not strong enough already in April, gave way beneath them. The remaining Teutonic villains found their graves at the bottom of the lake.

This historical event became the basis for Sergei Eisenstein's famous film, which played with great success a few years ago in the Soviet Union and, as far as I know, was favorably received in the United States. Setting about work with Eisenstein proved incredibly interesting, as he is not only a wonderful film director but also well-versed in music, as was evident in the very specific and descriptive musical tasks he gave me. It was likewise apparent in his insights concerning the music I composed. I requested that Eisenstein be present when it was recorded, as his observations were always very sensible.

After the film's premiere, I had the idea to use the music for a symphonic work with choir. Creating a cantata from the music was not an easy job, since it demanded considerably more effort than the original film composition. Most importantly, I needed to put the cantata on solid musical footing, to build it according to musical forms, to develop it symphonically, and then to re-orchestrate everything, since symphonic orchestration is a completely different thing than orchestration for a film. Despite my attempts to approach the music from a purely symphonic stand-point during this process, a certain element of visuality remained from the film and Eisenstein. Some musicians have objected to this visuality, but for others it facilitates the music's comprehension.

There are seven movements in the cantata. The first movement depicts Russia under the Mongolian yoke. Sorrowful melodies and the woodwinds sound as if they are telling the sad tale of Russia sinking under the weight of the Mongol Khans. The second movement is a song about Alexander Nevsky that gently tells of his victory over the Swedes at the Neva River. The third movement is the crusaders in Pskov. The clang of iron is heard as well as the gloomy singing of psalms, calling to mind the Inquisition and torture. They echo the cries of the women and children. The fourth movement is a short and energetic chorus: Arise, Ye Russian People. The people rise up in defense of their land. The fifth movement, the longest, depicts the Battle on Ice. At the beginning is an evocation of the lake and the cold, pre-dawn gloom. The crusaders' horns and the approaching clatter of hoofs are heard. Accompanied by the psalm singing, the Knights go on the attack and plow into the ranks of Russians. But a new musical element in D major appears: now Alexander's forces attack in turn. There is great confusion among the crusaders' ranks and the fanfares express the disorder on the lake. The sixth movement consists of a song intoned by a Russian girl who searches for her injured lover on the battlefield. The cantata concludes with the seventh movement, the entry of Alexander Nevsky into Pskov. Solemn and joyful songs mix with merry dances.

Alexander Nevsky said: he who comes to us with a sword shall die by the sword. On this stands Russia, and on this she shall stand forever. Fascist barbarians attacked the Soviet Union, hoping to enslave it. They miscalculated, and the entire Soviet people rose up and the enemy will be defeated. I am very pleased that my cantata will be performed during this time in the United States, our ally who fights alongside us for noble ideals and future peace.

ADDITIONAL SOURCES
FOR READING AND
LISTENING

THE CRITERION COLLECTION's *Eisenstein: The Sound Years* (2001) contains an excellent digital version of the 1986 Mosfilm restoration of *Alexander Nevsky*, conveniently boxed with both parts of Eisenstein's *Ivan the Terrible*. The collection also includes an audio essay on *Nevsky* by David Bordwell, the author of the most comprehensive and accessible study of Eisenstein's work, *The Cinema of Eisenstein* (Routledge, 2005). My own *Composing for the Red Screen: Prokofiev and Soviet Film* (Oxford University Press, 2013) traces Prokofiev's cinema work throughout the composer's career; chapter 4 offers a more rigorous musical analysis of *Nevsky* than the one in this book. For those interested in Prokofiev's biography, Harlow Robinson's *Sergei Prokofiev: A Biography* (Northeastern University Press, 2002), originally published in 1987, remains an eminently readable classic. Simon Morrison's *The People's Artist: Prokofiev's Soviet Years* (Oxford University Press, 2008), approaches the composer's later career from the perspective of newly available archival sources. A concise and excellent biography of Eisenstein is Oksana Bulgakowa's *Sergei Eisenstein: A Biography* (Potemkin, 2002).

A number of books provide further context. Marina Frolova-Walker's *Russian Music and Nationalism: From Glinka to Stalin* (Yale University Press, 2008) provides an essential prehistory to *Nevsky* by tracing the development of musical nationalism from its inception in the first half of the nineteenth century. Jay Leyda's *Kino: A History of the Russian and Soviet Film* (Princeton University Press, 1983) remains the classic, if now somewhat dated, survey of its subject. Those interested in the inner workings of Soviet film during the Stalin era will find much of interest in Jamie Miller's *Soviet Cinema: Politics and Persuasion under Stalin* (I. B. Tauris, 2010).

NOTES

CHAPTER 1

1 "Stalin Voted Third-Best Russian," *BBC News*, December 28, 2008, http://news.bbc.co.uk/2/hi/europe/7802485.stm, accessed February 2, 2016.

2 The page devoted to *Alexander Nevsky* on the *Name of Russia* website is at http://www.nameofrussia.ru/person.html?id=41, accessed February 2, 2016. Throughout this book, all translations from Russian are my own unless otherwise noted.

3 Quoted in Norman Swallow, *Eisenstein: A Documentary Portrait* (New York: Dutton, 1976), 123.

4 S. M. Eisenstein, "My Subject Is Patriotism," in *Selected Works. Writings, 1934–47*, ed. Richard Taylor, trans. William Powell (London: BFI, 1988), 118.

5 Quoted in Valentina Chemberdzhi, *XX vek Liny Prokof'evoi* (Moscow: Klassika-XXI, 2008), 184–85.

6 Izrail' Nest'ev, "Put' Sergeia Prokof'eva," in *Sovetskaia simfonicheskaia muzyka: sbornik statei*, ed. M. A. Grinberg (Moscow: Gosudarstvennoe muzykal'noe izdatel'stvo, 1955), 81–82. We will encounter Nest'ev's name frequently in this book; in the text I use the transliteration of his name (Israel Nestyev) that he himself used in his English-language publications.

7 David Ewen, *The Complete Book of 20th Century Music* (New York: Prentice-Hall, 1952), 292.

8 J. Peter Burkholder and Claude Palisca, *Norton Anthology of Western Music*, vol. 3, *Twentieth Century*, 6th ed. (New York: Norton, 2009), 317. On Socialist Realism, see Francis Maes, *A History of Russian Music: From Kamarinskaya to Babi Yar*, trans. Arnold J. Pomerans and Erica Pomerans (Berkeley: University of California Press, 2002), 255–70.

9 The transcript is in the Russian State Archive of Literature and Art, Moscow, Russia (hereafter RGALI), f. 2456, op. 1, ed. khr. 957, l. 23 (Galaktionov), f. 2456, op. 1, ed. khr. 957, l. 33 (Gorbatov).

10 Nicholas S. Timasheff, an émigré sociologist, coined the term "great retreat" in his *The Great Retreat: The Growth and Decline of Communism in Russia* (New York: E. P. Dutton, 1946).

11 Kevin M. F. Platt and David Brandenberger, "Tsarist-Era Heroes in Stalinist Mass Culture and Propaganda," in *Epic Revisionism: Russian History and Literature as Stalinist Propaganda*, ed. Kevin M. F. Platt and David Brandenberger (Madison: University of Wisconsin Press, 2006), 11.

12 On Soviet film and state legitimacy, see Jamie Miller, *Soviet Cinema: Politics and Persuasion under Stalin* (New York: I. B. Tauris, 2010). On the historical Alexander, see Mari Isoaho, *The Image of Aleksandr Nevskiy in Medieval Russia* (Boston: Brill, 2006).

13 The Politburo resolution is published in K. M. Anderson, ed., *Kremlevskii kinoteatr, 1928–1953: Dokumenty* (Moscow: ROSSPEN, 2005), 406.

14 Oksana Bulgakowa, *Sergei Eisenstein: A Biography*, trans. Anne Dwyer (San Francisco: Potemkin, 2001), 188. Peter Kenez surveys *Bezhin Meadow*'s production in "A History of Bezhin Meadow," in *Eisenstein at 100: A Reconsideration*, ed. Al Lavalley and Barry P. Scherr (New Brunswick, NJ: Rutgers University Press, 2001), 193–206.

15 The remarkable behind-the-scenes events leading up to the Politburo's vote on Eisenstein are charted in Anderson, *Kremlevskii kinoteatr*, 409–11, 417–20, 424. Jamie Miller discusses topical planning in *Soviet Cinema*, esp. 94.

16 "'Aleksandr Nevskii': Stakhanovskimi tempami. Opyt organizatsii podgotovitel'nykh rabot," *Kino*, July 5, 1938, 2.

17 Evgeny Dobrenko, *Stalinist Cinema and the Production of History: Museum of the Revolution*, trans. Sarah Young (New Haven, CT: Yale University Press, 2008), esp. 6–14.

18 James von Geldern, "Epic Revisionism and the Emergence of 'Public' Culture in the USSR," in Platt and Brandenberger, *Epic Revisionism*, 331.

19 Sergey Prokofiev, *Diaries, 1924–1933: Prodigal Son*, trans. Anthony Phillips (London: Faber & Faber, 2012), 195–96.

20 Ibid., 153.

21 Quoted in Harlow Robinson, ed. and trans., *Selected Letters of Sergei Prokofiev* (Boston: Northeastern University Press, 1998), 145–46.

22 Vernon Duke, *Passport to Paris* (Boston: Little, Brown, 1955), 175.

23 Andreas Huyssen, *After the Great Divide: Modernism, Mass Culture, Postmodernism* (Bloomington: Indiana University Press, 1986), vii.

24 Duke, *Passport to Paris*, 247.

25 Sergei Prokof'ev, *Dnevnik* (Paris: sprkfv, 2002), 2:756.

26 Ibid., 2:755–56.

27 Quoted in Bryan R. Simms, ed., *Composers on Modern Musical Culture: An Anthology of Readings on Twentieth-Century Music* (New York: Schirmer, 1999), 223.

28 S. S. Prokof'ev, "Puti sovetskoi muzyki," *Izvestiia*, November 16, 1934, 4.

29 On *Lieutenant Kijé*, see my "*Lieutenant Kizhe*: New Media, New Means," in *Prokofiev and His World*, ed. Simon Morrison (Princeton, NJ: Princeton University Press, 2008), 376–400.

30 Aaron Copland, *Our New Music* (New York: Whittlesey House, 1941), 121.

31 Stephen Press, *Prokofiev's Ballets for Diaghilev* (Burlington, VT: Ashgate, 2006).

32 Olin Downes, "Prokofiev Speaks: Russian Composer, Here This Week, Favors Return to Simpler, More Melodic Style," *New York Times*, February 2, 1930, 112.

33 Weill quoted in Richard Taruskin, *The Oxford History of Western Music*, vol. 5, *Music in the Early Twentieth Century* (New York: Oxford University Press, 2009), 534.

34 Chávez quoted in Howard Pollack, *Aaron Copland: The Life and Work of an Uncommon Man* (New York: Holt, 1999), 218.

35 Quoted in Simms, *Composers on Modern Musical Culture*, 224.

36 Taruskin, *Oxford History*, 5:775.

37 Marina Frolova-Walker, "The Glib, the Bland, and the Corny: An Aesthetic of Socialist Realism," in *Music and Dictatorship in Europe and Latin America*, ed. Roberto Illiano and Massimiliano Sala (Turnhout, Belgium: Brepols, 2009), 404.

38 Patrick Zuk, "Nikolay Myaskovsky and the 'Regimentation' of Soviet Composition: A Reassessment," *Journal of Musicology* 31 (2014): 354–93.

39 Viktor Varunts, ed., *Prokof'ev o Prokof'eve: Stat'i i interv'iu* (Moscow: Sovetskii kompozitor, 1999), 155.

40 Aaron Copland, *A Reader: Selected Writings 1923–1972*, ed. Richard Kostelanetz (New York: Routledge, 2004), 145.

41 Patrick Zuk argues that many of the fundamental tenets of Socialist Realism would have found widespread support outside the USSR in his "Soviet Music Studies outside Russia: Glasnost' and After," in *Russian Music Since 1917: Reappraisal and Rediscovery*, ed. Patrick Zuk and Marina Frolova-Walker (Oxford: Oxford University Press, forthcoming).

CHAPTER 2

1 "S. S. Prokof'ev i V. V. Alpers: Perepiska," in *Muzykal'noe nasledstvo: Sborniki po istorii muzykal'noi kul'tury SSSR*, ed. L. M. Kutateladze (Moscow: Gosudarstvennoe muzykal'noe izdatel'stvo, 1962), 1:431.

2 To cite just one of many examples, Ion Barna, an influential Eisenstein biographer, based his entire account of the collaboration on Eisenstein's own,

highly poeticized account (of which we will see more in chapter 5); see his *Eisenstein* (Bloomington: Indiana University Press, 1973), 214–18.

3 Gavriil Popov, *Iz literaturnogo naslediia: Stranitsy biografii*, ed. Z. A. Apetian (Moscow: Sovetskii kompozitor, 1986), 95.

4 Ibid., 262.

5 Quoted in David Bordwell, *The Cinema of Eisenstein* (New York: Routledge, 2005), 178.

6 Eisenstein first described a system of pre- and post-filming musical composition in a 1933 letter to Popov. RGALI f. 1923, op. 1, ed. khr. 1507, l. 1.

7 RGALI f. 1923, op. 1, ed. khr. 2047, ll. 5–6.

8 I. Romashchuk, *Gavriil Nikolaevich Popov: Tvorchestvo, vremia, sud'ba* (Moscow: Gosudarstvennyi muzykal'no-pedagogicheskii institut, 2000), 44–45.

9 Salaries for composers and directors were standardized in December 1938, apparently to correct large disparities in recent payments. For example, a director considered "first-rank" could be paid two thousand rubles per month of work (compare to Prokofiev's thirty-thousand-ruble honorarium). A. S. Deriabin, ed., *Letopis' rossiiskogo kino, 1930–1945* (Moscow: Materik, 2007), 587. Prokofiev's contract is in RGALI f. 1929, op. 1, ed. khr. 804, ll. 6–11; his payment of thirty thousand rubles is confirmed in a letter from the Mosfilm administration to Eisenstein, RGALI f. 1923, op. 1, ed. khr. 2640.

10 RGALI f. 1923, op. 1, ed. khr. 432, ll. 6–14.

11 These and the remaining quotes in this paragraph are from Prokofiev's annotated director's script, RGALI f. 1929, op. 1, ed. khr. 98.

12 A selection of Eisenstein's sketches is published in S. Eizenshtein, *Risunki* (Moscow: Iskusstvo, 1961).

13 S. Prokof'ev, "Moi novye raboty," *Literaturnaia gazeta*, September 20, 1938, 5.

14 These and the remaining quotes in this paragraph from RGALI f. 1929, op. 1, ed. khr. 98.

15 Prokofiev's contract indicates a June 10 deadline for the initial cues.

16 The conditions in Novgorod are described in Iu. V. Krivosheev and R. A. Sokolov, *Aleksandr Nevskii: Sozdanie kinoshedevra* (Saint Petersburg: Liki Rossii, 2012), 154; the subsequent construction at Mosfilm is detailed in "V studiiakh 'Aleksandr Nevskii': S'emki 'Ledovogo poboishcha,'" *Kino*, July 11, 1938, 4.

17 Krivosheev and Sokolov, *Aleksandr Nevskii*, 135.

18 E. Tissé, "S'emki na iskusstvennom l'du," *Kino*, October 23, 1938, 3.

19 Details in this paragraph come from Krivosheev and Sokolov, *Aleksandr Nevskii*, 158–60, as well as reports in *Kino* published on July 5 ("'Aleksandr Nevskii': Stakhanovskimi tempami," 2) and July 11 ("V studiiakh 'Aleksandr Nevskii': S'emki 'Ledovogo poboishcha,'" 4).

20 Tissé, "S'emki na iskusstvennom l'du."

21 The number of actors as given in "V studiiakh 'Aleksandr Nevskii'"; costume figures as given in Krivosheev and Sokolov, *Aleksandr Nevskii*, 170.

22 Ia. Kacher'ian, "Zakanchivaiutsia s'emki 'Aleksandra Nevskogo,'" *Kino*, September 23, 1938, 1.

23 Quoted in "'Aleksandr Nevskii': Stakhanovskimi tempami," among other articles.

24 "S. S. Prokof'ev i V. V. Alpers: Perepiska," 432. On the discrepancies between the musical plan and the completed film, see N. Rogozhina, "Muzyka 'Aleksandra Nevskogo' Prokof'eva v kinofil'me i kantate," in *Muzyka i sovremennost'* (Moscow: Gosudarstvennoe muzykal'noe izdatel'stvo, 1963), 2:114–15, 2:124–25. On Eisenstein and Prokofiev's work together, see Russell Merritt, "Recharging 'Alexander Nevsky': Tracking the Eisenstein-Prokofiev War Horse," *Film Quarterly* 48 (1995): 34–47.

25 On Prokofiev's blocking method, see my *Composing for the Red Screen: Prokofiev and Soviet Film* (New York: Oxford University Press, 2013), 70–71.

26 Aaron Copland, *Our New Music: Leading Composers in Europe and America* (New York: McGraw-Hill, 1941), 268–69.

27 On Prokofiev's reactions to Hollywood's time constraints, see Bartig, *Composing for the Red Screen*, 13.

28 Mikhail Rozenfel'd, "Aleksandr Nevskii," *Literaturnaia gazeta*, October 30, 1938, 6.

29 Sergei Prokof'ev, "Muzyka v fil'me *Aleksandr Nevskii*," in *Sovetskii istoricheskii fil'm: Sbornik statei*, ed. B. D. Grekov and E. Veisman (Moscow: Goskinoizdat, 1939), reprinted in S. I. Shlifshtein, ed., *S. S. Prokof'ev: Materialy, dokumenty, vospominaniia*, 2nd ed., (Moscow: Gosudarstvennoe muzykal'noe izdatel'stvo, 1961), 229.

30 Ibid., 229.

31 See, for instance, "'Alexander Nevsky' at Little," *Washington Post*, July 15, 1943, 21, and "Russian Film Has Premiere At the Little," *Washington Post*, July 27, 1939, 6.

32 On the early approval of *Nevsky*, see Krivosheev and Sokolov, *Aleksandr Nevskii*, 173.

33 Miller, *Soviet Cinema*, 127.

34 Prokof'ev, "Muzyka v fil'me *Aleksandr Nevskii*," 229.

35 Copland, *Our New Music*, 271.

36 Lydia Goehr, *The Imaginary Museum of Musical Works: An Essay in the Philosophy of Music* (New York: Oxford University Press, 1992), 222.

CHAPTER 3

1 The notes on the Catholic Mass are in RGALI f. 1923, op. 1, ed. khr. 459.

2 Vol'skii, "Vospominaniia o S. S. Prokof'eve," in Shlifshtein, *S. S. Prokof'ev*, 526.

3 The cue, in fact, parodies Igor Stravinsky's *Symphony of Psalms*; see Morag G. Kerr, "Prokofiev and His Cymbals," *Musical Times* 135 (1994): 608–9, and Bartig, *Composing for the Red Screen*, 83.

4 RGALI f. 1929, op. 2, ed. khr. 119.

5 The cues got their titles informally during the process of filming and editing; see Rogozhina, "Muzyka 'Aleksandra Nevskogo,'" 115.

6 Bordwell, *Cinema of Eisenstein*, 211.

7 R. Iurenev, *Sergei Eizenshtein: Zamysly, fil'my, metod* (Moscow: Iskusstvo, 1988), 2:169.

8 RGALI f. 2923, op. 1, ed. khr. 30, l. 17.5.

9 On the mixing of cues for the Battle on Ice, see Rogozhina, "Muzyka 'Aleksandra Nevskogo,'" 127.

10 Eisenstein, "My Subject Is Patriotism," 117.

11 M. Cheremukhin, "Muzyka k fil'mu 'Aleksandr Nevskii,'" *Kino-gazeta*, December 5, 1938, clipping in RGALI f. 1929, op. 1, ed. khr. 944.

12 On the Kuchka and the Russian sound, see Marina Frolova-Walker, *Russian Music and Nationalism from Glinka to Stalin* (New Haven, CT: Yale University Press, 2007), 52–73.

13 "Boundless steppe" quoted in Stuart Campbell, ed. and trans., *Russians on Russian Music, 1880–1917* (Cambridge, UK: Cambridge University Press, 2003), 92.

14 Lev Shvarts, "Muzyka fil'ma 'Aleksandr Nevskii,'" *Vecherniaia Moskva*, January 2, 1939, clipping in RGALI f. 1929, op. 1, ed. khr. 947, l. 3.

15 Prokof'ev, *Dnevnik*, 2:756.

16 Rogozhina details the relationship of film score and cantata in her "Muzyka 'Aleksandra Nevskogo,'"; a more meticulous charting is in Ulrich Wünschel, *Sergej Prokofjews Filmmusik zu Sergej Eisensteins* Alexander Newski (Hofheim, Germany: Wolke Verlag, 2006), 52–54. On the cantata's cultural context, see Vladimir Orlov, "Soviet Cantatas and Oratorios by Sergei Prokofiev in Their Social and Cultural Context" (Ph.D. diss., Cambridge University, 2010), 56–127.

17 Rogozhina, "Muzyka 'Aleksandra Nevskogo,'" 143.

18 Vol'skii, "Vospominaniia o S. S. Prokof'eve," 528. On Prokofiev's previous experiences with recording technology, see Bartig, *Composing for the Red Screen*, esp. 32.

19 Israel V. Nestyev, *Prokofiev*, trans. Florence Jonas (Stanford, CA: Stanford University Press, 1960), 299.

20 Quoted in Maes, *History of Russian Music*, 354.

CHAPTER 4

1 The admission ticket is in RGALI f. 1038, op. 1, ed. khr. 1235; quotations from the transcript of the discussion in RGALI f. 2923, op. 1, ed. khr. 30 and from the published review Vishnevsky based on his remarks, reprinted in *Sobranie sochinenii* (Moscow: Gosudarstvennoe izdatel'stvo khudozhestvennoi literatury, 1960), 5:422–25.

2 N. Kruzhkov, "Aleksandr Nevskii," *Pravda*, December 4, 1938, 4.

3 On historical inaccuracies, see David Brandenberger, "The Popular Reception of S. M. Eisenstein's *Aleksandr Nevskii*," in Platt and Brandenberger, *Epic Revisionism*, 233–52, esp. 235.

4 Prokofiev's contract is in RGALI f. 1929, op. 1, ed. khr. 804, ll. 6–11.

5 Announcements for the cantata began to appear in late January; see, for example, "Kantata 'Aleksandr Nevskii,'" *Sovetskoe iskusstvo*, January 25, 1939, 1.

6 In addition to the *Nevsky* Cantata (with V. A. Gagarina as soloist), the May 17, 1939, Moscow Philharmonic concert included Prokofiev's *Overture on Jewish Themes* and his Second Piano Concerto (program in RGALI f. 2985, op. 1, ed. khr. 654, ll. 24–25).

7 The manuscript of op. 78 is in RGALI f. 1929, op. 1, ed. khr. 251.

8 "45,000 zritelei fil'ma 'Aleksandr Nevskii,'" *Kino*, December 2, 1938, 1.

9 Harold Denny, "2 Soviet Notables Return to Favor," *New York Times*, December 5, 1938, 14.

10 Brandenberger, "The Popular Reception of S. M. Eisenstein's *Aleksandr Nevskii*," 246.

11 Prokofiev reports on *Periscope* in "Vecher S. Prokof'eva v Leningrade: Tvorcheskie plany kompozitora," *Vecherniaia Moskva*, January 5, 1939, clipping in RGALI f. 1929, op. 1, ed. khr. 947, l. 7.

12 Prokofiev's collaboration with Pronin announced in "Fil'm o progranichnikakh," *Vecherniaia Moskva*, January 25, 1939, clipping in RGALI f. 1929, op. 1, ed. khr. 947, l. 26.

13 The Dom Kino events are described in *Vecherniaia Moskva*, January 10, 1939, clipping in RGALI f. 1929, op. 1, ed. khr. 947, l. 12.

14 "Iz perepiski S. Prokof'eva i S. Eizenshteina," *Sovetskaia muzyka* 4 (1961): 106.

15 Quoted in Chemberdzhi, *XX vek Liny Prokof'evoi*, 201.

16 The Mosfilm administration clarified potential honoraria in a letter to Eisenstein, RGALI f. 1923, op. 1, ed. khr. 2640.

17 The *Nevsky* Cantata was performed twice at the *dekada*, the first directed by Lev Knipper, the second (an abridged version) under Prokofiev's direction. The musicologist Lev Danilevich reviewed the entire *dekada* for *Sovetskaia muzyka*, devoting a large section to the three cantatas. "Posle dekady," *Sovetskaia muzyka* 12 (1939), esp. 47–51.

18 I. Nest'ev, "Aleksandr Nevskii," *Sovetskoe iskusstvo*, May 27, 1939, 3.

19 Lev Shvarts, "Muzyka fil'ma 'Aleksandr Nevskii,'" *Vecherniaia Moskva*, January 2, 1939, clipping in RGALI f. 1929, op. 1, ed. khr. 947, l. 3.

20 S. Marich, "Zakliuchitel'nyi kontsert: Dekada sovetskoi muzyki," *Sovetskoe iskusstvo*, December 14, 1939, 2.

21 Nest'ev, "Aleksandr Nevskii," 3.

22 Shvarts, "Muzyka fil'ma 'Aleksandr Nevskii.'"

23 Vano Muradeli, "Novoe v sovetskoi muzyke," *Sovetskoe iskusstvo*, January 9, 1940, 2. In addition to Shostakovich, Boris Asaf'ev and Nikolai Miaskovsky had undergone similar *perestroiki* in 1933 and 1936, respectively.

24 Nest'ev, "Aleksandr Nevskii," 3.

25 Marich, "Zakliuchitel'nyi kontsert," 2.

26 D. Kabalevskii, "Zamysly i masterstvo," *Sovetskoe iskusstvo*, January 18, 1940, 2.

27 Marich, "Zakliuchitel'nyi kontsert," 2.

28 Nest'ev, "Aleksandr Nevskii," 3.

29 Marina Frolova-Walker, "'Music is obscure': Textless Soviet Works and Their Phantom Programmes," in *Representation in Western Music*, ed. Joshua S. Walden (Cambridge, UK: Cambridge University Press, 2013), 47–63.

30 Nest'ev, "Aleksandr Nevskii," 3.

31 Marian Koval', "Posle dekady," *Sovetskoe iskusstvo*, January 5, 1940, 5.

32 RGALI f. 2073, op. 1, ed. khr. 2, ll. 148–49.

33 RGALI f. 2073, op. 1, ed. khr. 2, l. 153.

34 RGALI f. 962, op. 10, ed. khr. 44, ll. 39–40.

35 Quoted in Jay Leyda, *Kino: A History of the Russian and Soviet Film* (London: Allen & Unwin, 1960), 365–66.

36 "Anti-German Films and a Play Are Withdrawn," *New York Times*, September 7, 1939, 3.

37 Krivosheev and Sokolov, *Aleksandr Nevskii*, 217.

38 "Uspekh sovetskikh kinofil'mov v Estonii," *Pravda*, May 24, 1940, 5.

39 Krivosheev and Sokolov, *Aleksandr Nevskii*, 215.

40 The English broadcast occurred on December 8, 1941. Styled as a radio drama, it featured the BBC Symphony and Chorus under the direction of Adrian Boult; see Edward Morgan, "Alexander Nevsky: A Play for Radio and a Prokofiev UK Première," *Three Oranges* 18 (2004), http://www.sprkfv.net/journal/three08/anevskyradio.html, accessed March 1, 2016.

41 RGALI f. 1929, op. 2, ed. khr. 119.

42 Ibid.

43 Olin Downes, "Stokowski Offers Prokofiev Work," *New York Times*, March 8, 1943, 10; P. B., "N.B.C. Orchestra Plays Prokofieff 'Nevsky' Score," *New York Herald Tribune*, March 8, 1943, 11.

44 Quotes from radio talk transcripts in the Olin Downes Papers, ms 688, Hargrett Library, University of Georgia, Athens (hereafter ODP), series 1, 14:5, 14:10, 14:19, 15:2.

45 Olin Downes, "Ormandy Offers Prokofieff Music," *New York Times*, April 4, 1945, 17.

46 Arthur Berger, "Music in Wartime," *New Republic*, February 7, 1944, 176.

47 Donald Fuller, "Russian and American Season, 1945," *Modern Music* 22 (May–June 1945): 254.

48 Paul Bowles, "Ormandy Leads Philadelphians in Final Concert," *New York Herald Tribune*, March 4, 1945, 11.

49 The recording was made on May 21, 1945, and first issued on Columbia Masterworks set M-580. It was reissued on LP as *Prokofiev, Alexander Nevsky cantata, op. 78* (The Philadelphia Orchestra / Eugene Ormandy / The Westminster Choir [with Jennie Tourel]), Columbia ML 4247, 1949. "Arise, Ye Russian People" circulated as early as 1942 on a rare collection ("Soviet Songs from Soviet Films") produced by the Stinson Trading Company. On radio broadcasts, see "Radio Programs of the Week" and similar listings in the *New York Times*, the *Washington Post*, and other major newspapers.

50 Mark A. Schubart, "Records," *New York Times*, December 9, 1945, 56.

51 Irving Kolodin, *The New Guide to Recorded Music* (Garden City, NY: Doubleday, 1950), 308.

52 The TASS report, dated April 7, is in RGALI f. 1929 op. 1, ed. khr. 947, l. 80.

53 *Serge Prokofieff, Alexander Nevsky, Cantata for Chorus and Orchestra* (New York: Leeds, 1945). The cantata had been published in the Soviet Union in 1941 by Muzgiz in a small print run; a second addition appeared in 1959 (*Aleksandr Nevskii: Kantata dlia metstso-soprano, khora i orkestra* [Moscow: Muzyka, 1959]), and six years later the work appeared in vol.16A of Prokofiev's collected works (*Sobranie sochinenii*, ed. N. P. Anosov [Moscow: Gosudarstvennoe muzykal'noe izdatel'stvo, 1965]). The 1945 publication appeared with astonishing speed; VOKS sent Helen Black the *Nevsky Cantata* score for publication only on April 3, 1945. State Archive of the Russian Federation, Moscow, Russia (hereafter GARF) f. 5283, op. 14, d. 246, l. 98.

54 Helen Black's letter of complaint, dated December 12, 1944, is in GARF f. 5283, op. 14, d. 246; the same file contains a copy of "Fight for Freedom."

55 "Soviet Seen Ready to Cooperate With U.S. on All Major Issues," *New York Times*, December 19, 1945, 15.

56 ODP Series 1, 44:10.

57 Olin Downes, "Composing in Wartime Russia," *New York Times*, December 23, 1945, 6X.

58 GARF f. 5283, op. 14, d. 278, l. 28.

59 GARF f. 5283, op. 14, d. 2, l. 165.

CHAPTER 5

1 Israel V. Nestyev, *Sergei Prokofiev: His Musical Life*, trans. Rose Prokofieva (New York: Knopf, 1946).

2 Izrail' Nest'ev, "O stile S. Prokof'eva," *Sovetskaia muzyka* 13 (1946). I am grateful to Daniel Tooke for introducing me to this review. Nestyev was likely influenced by the program note Dmitri Kabalevsky wrote for the premiere of Prokofiev's Fifth Symphony, in which he tried to demonstrate that the score evinced the positive qualities of Socialist Realism, including *narodnost'* (copy in RGALI f. 1929, op. 1, ed. khr. 906, ll. 6–10). I am grateful to Patrick Zuk for pointing out this connection.

3 Virgil Thomson, "Prokofieff in a New Mood," *New York Herald Tribune*, November 15, 1945. I am grateful to Daniel Tooke for sharing a copy of this review with me.

4 As translated in Alexander Werth, *Musical Uproar in Moscow* (London: Turnstile, 1949), 29. On the so-called Zhdanovshchina, see Maes, *History of Russian Music*, 308–17.

5 Werth, *Musical Uproar in Moscow*, 72.

6 On Nestyev's backtracking concerning the Sixth Symphony, see Nelli Kravets, *Riadom s velikami: Atovm'ian i ego vremia* (Moscow: GITIS, 2012), 284.

7 Nina Tumarkin, *The Living and the Dead: The Rise and Fall of the Cult of World War II in Russia* (New York: Basic Books, 1994), 8. On the front-line showings of *Nevsky*, see Rostislav Iurenev, "Aleksandr Nevskii," in *Rossiiskoe kino*, ed. L. M. Budiak (Moscow: Materik, 2003), 182.

8 See, for instance, Ivan Bol'shakov, "Tridtsat' let Sovetskogo kino," *Iskusstvo kino* 1 (February 1950): 4–7.

9 L. Shvarts, "O Sovetskoi kinomuzyke," *Iskusstvo kino* 3 (June 1948): 4–6.

10 T. Khrennikov, "Muzyka v kino," *Iskusstvo kino* 1 (February 1950): 26–28.

11 Piero Weiss and Richard Taruskin, eds., *Music in the Western World: A History in Documents* (New York: Schirmer, 1984), 426. The date of Stalin's death is contested in some circles; official word came on March 5.

12 Peter Schmelz, "After Prokofiev," in Morrison, *Prokofiev and His World*, esp. 503–7.

13 Grinberg, *Sovetskaia simfonicheskaia muzyka*, 270–74.

14 I. Nest'ev, "Put' Sergeia Prokof'eva," in ibid., 81–82.

15 M. Sabinina, "Vydaiushchiisia russkii kompozitor," *Sovetskaia kul'tura*, April 22, 1957, 4, and M. Sabinina, *Sergei Prokof'ev* (Moscow: Glavpoligrafproma, 1957), 48. Nestyev's assertions about Prokofiev's Third Piano Concerto are themselves likely derived from an earlier review by Boris Asaf'ev, "Tretii fortepiannyi kontsert Sergeia Prokof'eva," *Sovremennaia muzyka* 10 (1925): 57–63. I am grateful to Patrick Zuk for pointing me to this review.

16 B. Vol'skii, "Vospominaniia o S. S. Prokof'eve," 536.

17 Royal S. Brown, *Overtones and Undertones: Reading Film Music* (Berkeley: University of California Press, 1994), 134.

18 "Vertical Montage" first appeared in Sergei M. Eisenstein, *The Film Sense*, trans. and ed. Jay Leyda. (New York: Harcourt, Brace, 1942), 156–216. David Bordwell's study of Eisenstein's films and film theory, *The Cinema of Eisenstein*, remains the best and most accessible. See also Robert Robertson, *Eisenstein on the Audiovisual: The Montage of Music, Image and Sound in Cinema* (London: I. B. Tauris, 2009).

19 Theodor Adorno and Hanns Eisler, *Composing for the Films* (Atlantic Highlands, NJ: Athlon, 1994), 157.

20 Claudia Gorbman, *Unheard Melodies: Narrative Film Music* (Bloomington: Indiana University Press, 1987), 174n7. Nicholas Cook summarizes the criticism of Eisenstein's analysis in *Analysing Musical Multimedia* (Oxford: Clarendon, 1998), 57–65.

21 Quoted in M. Nest'eva and N. Kleiman, "Vydaiushchiisia khudozhnik-gumanist, *Sovetskaia muzyka* 9 (1979): 72.

22 Sergei Eisenstein, *The Eisenstein Collection*, ed. Richard Taylor (New York: Seagull, 2006), 151 (emphasis throughout is Eisenstein's). What Eisenstein calls "illustrative correspondence," often termed "Mickey-Mousing," was the subject of intense debate among Soviet film music composers during the 1930s. See my *"Kinomuzyka:* Theorizing Soviet Film Music in the 1930s," in *Sound, Speech, Music in Soviet and Post-Soviet Cinema*, ed. Masha Salazkina and Lilya Kaganovsky (Bloomington: Indiana University Press, 2014), 181–192.

23 S. M. Eizenshtein, *Izbrannye stat'i* (Moscow: Iskusstvo, 1956), 129–45; see my translation, "Sergey Eisenstein, 'PRKFV' (1947)," *Three Oranges: The Journal of the Serge Prokofiev Foundation* 30 (2015): 11–19.

24 Ibid., 14.

25 Prokof'ev, "Muzyka v fil'me *Aleksandr Nevskii*," 26–29.

26 Tatiana Egorova, *Soviet Film Music: An Historical Survey*, trans. Tatiana A. Ganf and Natalia A. Egunova (Amsterdam: Harwood, 1997), 60.

27 Ibid., 67.

28 John Riley, *Dmitri Shostakovich: A Life in Film* (London: I. B. Tauris, 2005), 34.

29 Brown, *Overtones and Undertones*, 134. The questionable source is Barna, *Eisenstein*, 216.

30 David Nice describes this film spot in his blog; see "Electric *Nevsky*," July 22, 2011, http://davidnice.blogspot.com/2011/07/electric-nevsky.html, accessed August 1, 2014.

31 Sergei Morozov, *Prokof'ev* (Moscow: Molodaia gvardiia, 1967), 201.

32 I. Nest'ev. *Zhizn' Sergeia Prokof'eva*, 2nd ed. (Moscow: Kompozitor, 1973), 424.

33 Nestyev, *Sergei Prokofiev*, 158.

34 Rebecca Schwartz-Bishir, "Aleksandr Nevskiy: Prokofiev's Successful Compromise with Socialist Realism," in *Composing for the Screen in Germany and the USSR*, ed. Phil Powrie and Robynn Stilwell (Bloomington: Indiana University Press, 2007), 148–60.

35 Gerald Abraham, *Eight Soviet Composers* (New York: Oxford University Press, 1943), 32.

36 Ibid., 42.

37 Andrey Olkhovsky, *Music under the Soviets: The Agony of an Art* (New York: Praeger, 1955), 166.

38 Ibid., 167.

39 Claude Samuel, *Prokofiev* (Paris: Éditions du Seuil, 1960); the quotation is from Miriam John's English translation (New York: Marion Boyars, 2000), 139.

40 Lawrence Hanson and Elisabeth Hanson, *Prokofiev, the Prodigal Son: An Introduction to His Life and Work in Three Movements* (London: Cassell, 1964), 176.

41 Liner notes to *Prokofieff: Alexander Nevsky* (Chicago Symphony Orchestra/ Fritz Reiner), RCA Victor Red Seal LM-2395, 1960.

42 Victor Seroff, *Sergei Prokofiev: A Soviet Tragedy* (New York: Funk & Wagnalls, 1968); quotes are from the 1969 English edition (London: Leslie Frewin), 250 (emphasis mine).

43 Ibid., 255.

44 Stanley D. Krebs, *Soviet Composers and the Development of Soviet Music* (New York: Norton, 1970), 154.

45 Arthur Berger, "Prodigal Son," *New York Review of Books*, October 22, 1987, http://www.nybooks.com/articles/1987/10/22/prodigal-son/, accessed April 6, 2016.

46 Danielle Fosler-Lussier, *Music Divided: Bartók's Legacy in Cold War Culture* (Berkeley: University of California Press, 2007).

47 Liner notes to *Sergei Prokofiev: Alexander Nevsky and War and Peace (Highlights)* (USSR Academic Symphony Orchestra / Republican Russian Chorus / Yevgeni Svetlanov [first work]; Bolshoi Theater Orchestra and Soloists / Alexander Melik-Pashayev [second work]), Musical Heritage Society 824351, 1981; the release was a reissue of Svetlanov's 1966 recording.

CHAPTER 6

1 Anthony Burgess, *On Mozart: A Paean for Wolfgang* (New York: Ticknor & Fields, 1991), 6.

2 Maria Biesold, *Sergej Prokofjew: Komponist im Schatten Stalins* (Berlin: Quadriga, 1996), 239–40.

3 On the German premiere see Frit'of Ben'iamin Shenk, *Aleksandr Nevskii v russkoi kul'turnoi pamiati: Sviatoi, pravitel', natsional'nyi geroi (1263– 2000)*, trans. Elena Zemskovaia and Maiia Lavrinovich (Moscow: Novoe Literaturnoe Obozrenie, 2007), 391n326.

4 This paragraph is summarized from Stephen Lloyd, *William Walton: Muse of Fire* (Rochester, NY: Boydell, 2001), 196–98; Neil Tierney, *Sir William Walton: His Life and Music* (London: Hale, 1984), 108–10; and Michael Kennedy, *Portrait of Walton* (New York: Oxford University Press, 1989), 124–25.

5 On the ethics debates surrounding *Carmina Burana*, see Michael H. Kater, *Composers of the Nazi Era* (New York: Oxford University Press, 2001), esp. 111–14.

6 Jacques Ellul, *Propaganda: The Formation of Men's Attitudes*, trans. Konrad Kellen and Jean Lerner (New York, Knopf, 1965).

7 Richard Taruskin, "Prokofiev, Hail … and Farewell?," *New York Times*, April 21, 1991, 25.

8 Ibid.

9 Details in this paragraph summarized from William Brohn's email communication with the author, May 21, 2016. The score for *Alexander Nevsky* does not survive in its entirety. The version that was used during recording and presumably deposited in Mosfilm's archives has disappeared, likely lost or destroyed when the studio was evacuated during the Second World War. A partial orchestral score is in RGALI f. 1929, op. 1, ed. khr. 96.

10 Goberman as quoted in liner notes to *Alexander Nevsky* (Saint Petersburg Philharmonic Orchestra / Yuri Temirkanov), Sony 09026-61926-2, 1993.

11 John Henken, "Rescoring 'Alexander Nevsky': Would Prokofiev Roll Over?," *Los Angeles Times*, November 1, 1987, K64.

12 Valerie Cruice, "Prokofiev's 'Nevsky' For Music Video Fans," *New York Times*, September 16, 1990, CN22.

13 Edward Rothstein, "Eisenstein's 'Nevsky,' Ozawa and the Bostonians," *New York Times*, October 28, 1991, C13.

14 Joseph McLellan, "The NSO's Recharged 'Nevsky,'" *Washington Post*, August 28, 1989, B1.

15 Joseph McLellan, " 'Nevsky': NSO at the Movies," *Washington Post*, August 4, 1990, G5.

16 The cost of the initial performances as given in Daniel Cariaga, " 'Alexander Nevsky' Reborn," *Los Angeles Times*, November 5, 1987, E1.

17 Quoted in Howard Reich, " 'Nevsky' Finally Thaws Out," *Chicago Tribune*, April 26, 1987, L22.

18 Quotes and details in this paragraph from Jon Burlingame, "Score One for Movie Maestros: Audiences Grow for Film-Music Concerts," *Variety*, November 12, 2013, available online at http://variety.com/2013/biz/news/

score-one-for-movie-maestros-audiences-grow-for-film-music-concerts-1200827772/, accessed May 17, 2016.

19 Krivosheev and Sokolov, *Aleksandr Nevskii*, 228.

20 Quoted in Vita Ramm, "Rezhisser fil'ma 'Aleksandr. Nevskaia bitva' Igor' Kalenov: 'Eto fil'm o mal'chike, kotoryi vstupaet v rukovodstvo stranoi,'" *Izvestiia*, April 11, 2008, 1.

21 Larisa Maliukova, "'Aleksandr. Nevskaia Bitva': Nash Remiek 1938-go," *Novaia gazeta*, May 8, 2008, 19–20.

22 Eisenstein's production of *Die Walküre* premiered at the Bolshoi on November 21, 1940, and had six performances in total. On the production, see Rosamund Bartlett, "The Embodiment of Myth: Eizenshtein's Production of *Die Walküre*," *Slavonic and East European Review* 70 (1992): 53–76. The festival of "German-Russian Cultural Meetings" took place in 2003–4; among its initiatives was a booklet that accompanied the film-concert, *S. Eizenshtein/S. Prokof'ev: V ramkakh Rossiisko-Germanskikh kul'turnykh vstrech 2004* (Moscow: Goethe-Institut, 2004).

23 Wünschel, *Sergej Prokofjews Filmmusik*, 64–66.

24 "Fil'm-kontsert 'Aleksandr Nevskii' v Bol'shom teatre: Pervye vpechatleniia. 'Kruglyi stol' v Muzee kino," *Kinovedcheskie zapiski* 70 (2004), available online at http://www.kinozapiski.ru/ru/article/sendvalues/216/, accessed November 9, 2015.

25 Ibid.

26 Ibid.

27 Ekaterina Chen, "Saundtrek: Skrestili mechi so smychkami," *Gazeta*, November 29, 2004, 15.

28 Ekaterina Biriukova, "Nemtsy ozhivili russkogo sviatogo: 'Aleksandr Nevskii' v Bol'shom teatre," *Izvestiia*, November 30, 2004, 11.

29 Varvara Turova, "Kontsert kinomuzyka: Nemets vyigral Ledovoe poboishche," *Kommersant*, November 29, 2004, 21.

30 Ibid.

31 Svetlana Samoilova, "Khvala nemetskoi dotoshnosti: 'Aleksandr Nevskii' zazvuchal po-prokof'evski," *Vremia novostei*, November 29, 2004, 10.

APPENDIX

1 RGALI f. 1929 op. 2 ed. khr. 119. The translation is my own.

INDEX

Nestyev, Israel, 5, 67–68, 75, 76–77, 78, 79, 80, 87, 97, 98–99, 100–1, 102, 103, 108–9, 115, 141n6, 150n2, 150n15
New England Patriots, 123
New York Herald Tribune, 84, 87, 113
New York Times, 19, 73, 81, 84, 88, 92, 124
Nice, David, 108

Olivier, Laurence: *Henry V*, 121–22
Olkhovsky, Andrey: *Music under the Soviets: The Agony of an Art*, 110–12
Oppenheim Family, The, 81
Order of Alexander Nevsky, 99
Order of Saint Alexander Nevsky, 132
Orff, Carl: *Carmina Burana*, 123
Ormandy, Eugene, 85, 88, 89, 93

Paramount Studios, 30
Pasolini, Pier Paolo: *Gospel According to St. Matthew*, 6
patriotism, 4, 10, 13, 47, 56, 57, 61, 64, 86, 88, 96, 112, 114, 115, 117, 123, 129, 132, 133
Pavlenko, Petr, 3, 12, 31, 70
perestroika, 77, 78, 148n23
Periscope, 74
Peter I, 9, 11
Peter the Great, 10, 11
Philadelphia Orchestra, 85, 88
Platt, Kevin, 11
Politburo, 12
Popov, Gavriil, 27–30 (*see also* composer-director collaboration)
First Symphony, 30
Pravda, 9, 70, 75, 77, 82

Press, Stephen, 19
Previn, Andre, 125, 127, 129
Professor Mamlok, 81
Prokofiev, Sergei (*see also* composer-director collaboration)
and ballet, 15, 18, 19, 26, 32–33, 64–65
"light-serious" music, *see* simplification of musical style
and mass audiences, 7, 16–19, 63–64, 83–84 (*see also* accessibility)
opinion of film music, 15–16, 73–75
simplification of musical style, 18–19
WORKS (*see also Alexander Nevsky*)
Ala and Lolli, 64
Cantata for the Twentieth Anniversary of October, 66, 111
Chout (ballet and suite), 65
Fifth Symphony, 97, 150n2
First Symphony ("The Classical"), 88
Fourth Symphony, 78
Lieutenant Kijé (film score and suite), 18, 19, 41, 65, 106
Peter and the Wolf, 105
Romeo and Juliet (ballet and suites), 33, 65
Scythian Suite, 65, 76
Sixth Symphony, 98–99
Songs of Our Days, 22
Sur le Borysthène, 18
Third Piano Concerto, 88, 101, 150n15
Third Symphony, 78
War and Peace, 97
Zdravitsa, 66, 111, 115

Pronin, Vasily: *Commandant of Bird Island*, 74
propaganda, 8–14, 27, 38–40, 45, 72, 81–82, 85, 107–9, 110, 111–15, 121–24, 128, 129
Pudovkin, Vsevolod, 54
Pushkin, Alexander, 10–11
Putin, Vladimir, 4, 130

Rabinowitz, Peter J., 117
Rachel Maddow Show, The, 123
Rachmaninov, Sergei, 17
Raimi, Sam: *Darkman*, 6
RCA Victor, 6, 113, 114, 115
Reiner, Fritz, 6, 113
Revolution, Russian, 7, 10, 12, 66, 116
Riley, John, 107
Rimsky-Korsakov, Nikolai, 22, 61, 75, 78, 122
  Legend of the Invisible City of Kitezh, The, 54, 79
  Sadko, 62, 110
  Snow Maiden, The, 59–60
Robinson, Harlow, 116
Roman Catholicism, 47, 49
Romantic musical values, 16, 29, 78, 96, 110, 112, 120
Romm, Mikhail, 3, 12
Roosevelt, Theodore, 82
Rostropovich, Mstislav, 125
Rothstein, Edward, 127
Rozenfeld, Mikhail, 43
Russian Civil War, 74
Russian Ministry of Culture, 131
Russian Orthodoxy, 47, 132

Sabinina, Marina, 101
Sam Fox (publishing house), 90
Samoilova, Svetlana, 133
Samuel, Claude, 112
Schmelz, Peter, 100

Schoenberg, Arnold:
  Gurrelieder, 65
Schubert, Mark, 88
Schwartz-Bishir, Rebecca, 109
Scriabin, Alexander, 105
Second World War, 2, 7, 22, 68, 72, 92, 93, 97, 99, 110, 114
serialism, *see* dodecaphony
Seroff, Victor: *Sergei Prokofiev: A Soviet Tragedy*, 113–115
Sevastopol, Siege of, 6, 101
Shaporin, Yuri, 75, 76, 77
  On Kulikovo Field, 76
Shostakovich, Dmitri, 68, 77, 85, 100, 107
  Fifth Symphony, 68, 77
  Seventh Symphony, 84
Shvarts, Lev, 44, 63, 75, 77, 99–100
Sikorski, 133
Simpsons, The, 123
Socialist Realism, 7, 20, 22, 52, 64, 79, 97, 98, 102, 103, 109, 133, 143n41, 150n2
sonata form, 67–68
Soviet All-Union Society for Cultural Ties Abroad, *see* VOKS
Soviet Literature, 43
Soviet Symphonic Music, 100
sovremennost, *see* contemporaneity
Spielberg, Steven: *Jaws*, 6
Stakhanov, Aleksei, 39
Stakhanovism, 39, 43, 102
Stalin Era, 4, 23, 44, 55–56, 76, 129, 130, 131
Stalin, Joseph, 1, 2, 3, 10, 12, 13, 14, 66, 80, 99, 100, 111, 115, 119, 127, 133
Stalin Prize, 80–81, 82
Stalinism, 8, 27, 123, 124, 127, 128

Stasov, Vladimir, 75
Stokowski, Leopold, 84, 90, 92
Stravinsky, Igor, 85, 87
  Firebird, The, 116
  Petrushka, 116
  Symphony of Psalms, 87
Strobel, Frank, 130–31, 132, 133
Suvorov, 73
Svetlanov, Evgeny, 117
Swanson, Gloria, 17, 30, 31

Taruskin, Richard, 100, 123–24
TASS, 89
Tchaikovsky, Peter, 54–55, 98
  1812 Overture, 54
Tcherepnin, Nikolai, 15, 16
Thaw, The, 96, 100
Thomson, Virgil, 97
Tissé, Eduard, 3, 36, 38, 40, 43, 102
Tourel, Jennie, 90
Tsukkerman, Viktor, 74
Tumarkin, Nina, 99
Turova, Varvara, 133

Vasnetsov, Viktor, 76
Verdi, Giuseppe, 58, 61
Vishnevsky, Vsevolod, 69–70
visuality, 51, 52, 68, 79–80, 83–84,
  87, 105
VOKS, 83, 84, 89, 90, 92
Volsky, Boris, 48, 49, 102

Wagner, Richard, 58, 105, 119
  Walküre, Die, 131
Walton, William: Score for *Henry V*,
  121–123
Warhol, Andy, 88, 89
Washington Post, 127
Webern, Anton: cantatas, 65–66
Weill, Kurt, 19
Westminster Choir, 84
What a Widow!, 17
Wilson, John, 129
work concept, 45, 126

Zhdanov, Andrei, 98
Zhdanov resolution, 97–98, 102